PRIMO LEVI AND THE IDENTITY OF A SURVIVOR

Primo Levi (1919–1987) was an Italian chemist, writer, and Holocaust survivor who used a combination of testimony, essays, and creative writing to explore crucial themes related to the Shoah. His voice is among the most important to emerge from this dark chapter in human history.

In *Primo Levi and the Identity of a Survivor*, Nancy Harrowitz examines the complex role that Levi's Jewish identity played in his choices of how to portray his survival, as well as in his exposition of topics such as bystander complicity. Her analysis uncovers a survivor's shame that deeply influenced the personas he created to recount his experiences. Exploring a range of Levi's works, including *Survival in Auschwitz* and lesser-known works of fiction and poetry, she illustrates key issues within his development as a writer. At the heart of Levi's discourse, Harrowitz argues, lies a complex interplay of narrative modes that reveals his brilliance as a theorist of testimony.

(Toronto Italian Studies)

NANCY HARROWITZ is an associate professor of Italian and Jewish studies at Boston University.

PRIMO LEVI

AND THE IDENTITY OF A SURVIVOR

NANCY HARROWITZ

UNIVERSITY OF TORONTO PRESS

Toronto Buffalo London

© University of Toronto Press 2017
Toronto Buffalo London
www.utorontopress.com
Printed and bound by CPI Group (UK) Ltd, Croydon, CR0 4YY

Reprinted in paperback 2018

ISBN 978-1-4875-0102-0 (cloth)   ISBN 978-1-4875-2328-2 (paper)

♾ Printed on acid-free, 100% post-consumer recycled paper

(Toronto Italian Studies)

Library and Archives Canada Cataloguing in Publication

Harrowitz, Nancy A. (Nancy Anne), 1952–, author
Primo Levi and the identity of a survivor / Nancy Harrowitz.

(Toronto Italian studies)
Includes bibliographical references and index.
ISBN 978-1-4875-0102-0 (cloth).   ISBN 978-1-4875-2328-2 (softcover)

1. Levi, Primo–Criticism and interpretation.   I. Title.
II. Series: Toronto Italian studies

PQ4872.E8Z75 2017   853'.914   C2016-904898-5

A portion of chapter 3 (pp. 67–81) is a revised version of a chapter originally published as "Mon Maître, Mon Monstre" in *Monsters in the Italian Literary Imagination*, ed. Keala Jewell (Detroit: Wayne State University Press, 2011), pp. 51–62.

University of Toronto Press acknowledges the financial assistance to its publishing program of the Canada Council for the Arts and the Ontario Arts Council, an agency of the Government of Ontario.

 Canada Council **Conseil des Arts**
for the Arts   du Canada

 ONTARIO ARTS COUNCIL
CONSEIL DES ARTS DE L'ONTARIO
an Ontario government agency
un organisme du gouvernement de l'Ontario

Funded by the   Financé par le
Government   gouvernement
of Canada   du Canada

 Canadä

To my mother, Irene Harrowitz, who taught me the meaning of persistence

Contents

Contents

Acknowledgments

There are many in the community of Levi scholars to whom I owe much for animated conversation and intellectual stimulation. First and foremost are the members of an informal Primo Levi scholars group who regularly organized conference panels and lectures together over the past ten or more years: Risa Sodi, whose significant early work on Levi was an inspiration; Penny Marcus, who together with Risa organized an important conference on Levi at Yale and who has written beautifully on Levi; Robert Gordon and Joe Farrell, both major forces in Levi studies; and Jonathan Druker, Stan Pugliese, Sharon Portnoff, and Berel Lang, all of whom have not only written essential works on Levi but organized and participated in those scholarly events that inspired further study of this important author. I've had countless thought-provoking conversations over the years with them and owe them a large debt of gratitude for their stimulating work in this field. My department and college at Boston University have also been unstintingly supportive of my research.

To my other friends, who read chapters and made a real impact on my work, in particular Melissa Zeiger, Beth Goldsmith, Fiora Bassanese, and Keala Jewell: life would have been so much harder without your encouraging words. And finally, to my husband August Watters, who supported this project and played so much sweet music in the background.

PRIMO LEVI AND THE IDENTITY OF A SURVIVOR

Introduction

Despite the passage of more than seventy years since the Shoah and several decades since his death, the voice and philosophical perspectives of the Holocaust survivor and writer Primo Levi have intensified in importance.[1] Much has been written on and about him, in an impressive variety of fields that range from history to literature to trauma studies. Called a "natural philosopher" by Berel Lang, Levi is widely recognized as a profound and wise voice, but the mechanisms through which he communicates his wisdom and many of the ramifications of his thought are sometimes missed, as well as the relationship between key elements of his work.

Levi's identity as a survivor and as a writer emerges within the constraints of an autobiographical mode that he seems to find highly problematic. The project of autobiography, telling his own story, is often delegated to the background in Levi's writing in order to pursue the communal subject. He employs diverse strategies to ensure that the autobiographical subject appears as secondary, so that the vision of the world is foregrounded over a vision of the self. The exploration of the self commonly found in autobiography becomes instead an investigation of the damage done to the self by the experience of the camp.

A principal goal of this study is to examine the multifaceted nexus of autobiography, testimony, and creative writing in Levi's work, through an understanding of the complex role that his cultural identity played in his choices of who and what to foreground in that work. In order to address the Shoah, the exigencies of testimony must trump those of autobiography, and yet the literariness of Levi's writings pulls in another direction, that of telling the best story possible. Exploring the tensions between these modes reveals the backdrop of shame that lies behind his survivor's experience, permeating his texts and deeply influencing his creation of writing personas through which to recount his story. The heart of Levi's discourse lies in this agonistic arena, as well as his brilliance as a theorist of testimony.

I explore some very different texts of Levi's to examine how he established his identity as a survivor within the exigencies of telling his life story, looking at his decisions about which stories to tell and precisely how to tell them. The choice of texts to examine is meant as strategic rather than comprehensive, as my goal is to illustrate key issues within Levi's development as a writer. The texts I discuss range from his best known, namely his testimonial and semi-testimonial works, to lesser known fiction and poetry.

I contend that in order to understand the relationship between these three modes that are so fundamental to his work, the role of his various cultural identities must be examined, each in their own context. A crucial but missing piece in much current Levi scholarship has been precisely this understanding of the relationship of his complicated cultural identities to his textual production and to the literariness of his work. The articulation of that relationship forms an integral part of his thought, as well as of the way he expresses some of his more urgent themes in his opus.

Levi had a multifaceted cultural identity that could be better described as a set of identities. He was Italian, a trained chemist, a member of Turin's Jewish community, a survivor of Auschwitz, and an immensely talented writer, who eventually retired early from his job as the manager of a paint factory so as to have more time to devote to the craft of writing. The relationships between various aspects of his identities and his work are intricate and delicate. Each self carries with it its own set of exigencies and sub-identities; each produces different expressions within various genres of his work, and at times those articulations can be contradictory and deep in their interactions. An examination of the implications and effects of these sometimes competing and even incompatible identities reveals what is rich and original about Levi's thought. The categories of "Levi the scientist," "Levi the survivor and testimonial writer," and even "Levi the assimilated Jew" have become convenient classifications within which he has often been pigeonholed, and the lack of dialogue between these categories has been detrimental to understanding his work.

Critics and readers have often overlooked the astonishing depth of Levi's work for these and other reasons; they have tended to read

Levi quite literally, without exploring what his literary strategies are and how he structures his texts. A related concern that has affected the reception of his texts is the common assumption that Holocaust testimony is or should be entirely transparent in its communication with the reader: that literary structures either are not part of testimony or should not be, that their coexistence in the same text is contradictory or problematic. This assumption leads to a tendency to take the author at his or her word about the meaning of his texts and to look no further, especially in the case of an author as articulate as Levi. As Jonathan Druker comments, "to date, nearly all Levi scholarship approaches this major and literary ethical figure within the terms of his own discourse."[2] If one does not look beyond Levi's own statements, much indeed goes unnoticed. This seems obvious, yet this myopic view has been the case with much of Levi scholarship and has influenced the reception of his texts by a larger audience as well. James Young comments that "ultimately all writers of objective or factual narrative assert at least two kinds of significance: that in the way they represent events and that in a style that represents itself as style-less."[3] It is Levi's purported "style-lessness" that has been at issue: the role of style has been largely unacknowledged as a major factor in the production of meaning in his texts.

Another of the goals of my study, as well as its principal methodology, is to look at how Levi's texts generate their significance, through an examination of the literary strategies that he employs. The first step in this endeavour, as obvious as it may seem, is to look beyond what he himself says about writing and about his texts. The neglect of much close interpretation of Levi's texts is puzzling, because his writing is so powerful and his influence so widespread that his work has become central to the study of the Shoah.[4] The reasons for his tremendous impact merit a close investigation in order to more fully understand his extraordinary legacy. A major focus of this book is thus to examine how and why he arrives at such an impact, through close readings of the literariness of his work.

The initial chapters of this study follow in a roughly chronological fashion the development and itinerary of Levi's most important cultural identities. Chapter 2 begins with the construction of Jewish identity in post-unification nineteenth-century Italy, as a preamble to a discussion of Levi's own Jewish identity. This may seem a long way from the historical period in which Levi lived, but Jewish responses to the 1860–1861 unification of Italy, which included the abolishment of the ghettos before and after these dates, and ensuing changes in the composition of Italian Jewish identities determined to a large extent the outlook and attitudes of Levi's generation. This patriotic response is one of the reasons why Levi, along with so many of his contemporaries, largely rejected the reality of Italy's clearly antisemitic policies. Their beloved Italy was not recognizable in fascism, even though the warning signs had been there for a quite a while, beginning with antisemitic press in the late 1920s, leading to the racial laws of 1938 that marginalized Italian Jews and stripped them of their civil rights as citizens, finally culminating in shameful episodes after the German invasion of 1943 in which Italian fascists help deport Italian Jews to their deaths.[5]

The chapter then turns to what Levi's Jewish identity meant to him and how he represented it in interviews, essays, and his other writing. Full of reversals and some intriguing contradictions, the interplay between Levi's Jewish identity and his Italian identity was thorny, and this complexity reveals itself in some arresting textual moments discussed in this chapter. Did the assertion of one of these identities imply a loss, real or imagined, of the other? What was the effect of the enforced identity of persecution on his deeply felt nationalism as an Italian? And finally, what were the effects of his Jewish identity on his self-representation as a writer? Levi's position on his Jewishness has been enigmatic, both for himself and for his readers and critics. During his lifetime, he made differing statements about this identity, ranging from an interview in which he asserted a strong Jewish identity to statements that strongly underplay the Jewish part of his identity in favour of the Italian component. How these different and often contradictory positions on his Jewish identity interact, and what they imply about a specifically Italian Jewish identity, are compelling matters not only for what they say about Levi himself, but for the story they tell regarding a post-Holocaust crisis of Jewish identity.

Exploration of these questions and others leads to further questions about Levi's identity as a writer. This is the topic of chapter 3, which explores Levi's self-creation as a writer, how his self-representation has been read, and the implications therein for understanding his texts and their impact. In general, Levi's biographers have portrayed him as an intensely private and shy individual who spoke only rarely and circumspectly about personal matters in his writing. His literary voice, however, is strong and self-assured, using an arsenal of literary techniques that range from profound employments of classical traditions to a deep and penetrating irony.[6] The story of Levi's writerly vocation begins with his first published work, a report on the sanitary conditions of

Auschwitz that he co-authored with fellow prisoner Leonardo Debenedetti in a medical journal. Druker has stated that "Levi the survivor is
a narrating persona that cannot simply be equated with the chemist,
writer, and Holocaust survivor named Primo Levi."[7] This assertion is
certainly accurate; and the issues related to his multiple identity formations have also created multiple narrating personas, as I discuss in this
chapter. Michel Foucault's dictum "One writes in order to become other
than what one is"[8] suggests that autobiography, for example, offers an
opportunity for self-transformation. In Levi's case that transformation
was tremendously liberating, as it allowed him to create various writing personas that could go beyond the strictures of his shyness and of
his career as a manager of a paint factory, a job that did offer occasional
intellectual challenges but certainly did not provide the kind of intellectual stimulation that Levi was able to achieve as an author.

The notion of a writing persona itself raises an interesting yet thorny
issue: Does Levi write testimony in order to become "other" to his
damaged, converted self? In his creation of the persona who testifies,
who narrates, the damage is apparent, but the act of writing is healing, as he has alluded to many times in his opus. Can the protection
that the distance of the writing persona affords work towards healing
in a different way than Levi explains? The model of the conversation
narrative is helpful in understanding the subject position of a survivor who writes about his or her experiences. The "old" self is the one
who journeys through the traumatic temporal history, what Lawrence
Langer has called "durational time."[9] The "new" self is the one who has
been permanently and profoundly altered by the experience and who
writes about it afterwards, from the subject position of the survivor: a
changed self, now a writer, who must deal with the after-effects of the
dehumanization suffered in the camps. A compelling example of the
split between the old and the new self is found at the very end of Elie
Wiesel's *Night*, after Wiesel is freed, as the survivor gazes upon himself
for the first time since deportation:

> One day when I was able to get up, I decided to look at myself in the
> mirror on the opposite wall. I had not seen myself since the ghetto.
> From the depths of the mirror, a corpse was contemplating me.
> The look in his eyes as he gazed at me has never left me.[10]

It is the old self who attempts to see himself in the mirror, and the
new self, dead in relation to the old self, who gazes back. In Wiesel's

articulation, that look which represents the effect of the dehumanization suffered in the camp is now a permanent part of the self. This shocking moment of assessment brings to bear the tremendous discrepancy between selves: who he was before deportation, and who he is now. The new self's act of contemplating the old underscores the differences: does the new self even recognize himself in the old? And how will the two coexist, now that the existence of that changed self has been glimpsed?

The model of the conversion of the self is particularly well articulated in Dante studies. In the terminology that is often used, Dante the pilgrim is the old self who is lost, and who journeys though hell, purgatory, and paradise as a pedagogical and spiritual exercise, learning about sin, its ramifications, and redemption along the way. Dante the poet is the figure that writes so compellingly after the end of the journey about these imaginary experiences and the salvation that ultimately comes with them. Dante as an actor in his own drama is the old self; the perspective created by distance afterwards creates Dante the poet. As Levi was such a devoted student of Dante, this metaphor is particularly useful in looking at the new self – the writerly identity – that Levi has forged out of his experience. Much interesting scholarly work has been done on the frequent references to Dante in Levi's writings, and an exposition of the episode in which Levi cites canto 26 to a fellow prisoner is included in my discussion of Levi's self-creation as a writer in chapter 3. The irreconcilable difference in their situations is, of course, that Dante the poet is healed at the end of his fictive journey, as he has seen Paradise. Levi the newly forged poet, however, never really makes it out of hell, as the hell of Auschwitz is profoundly damaging and the effects permanent. As Sharon Portnoff comments in her astute analysis of the relationship of Levi's testimony to Dante, "Levi's use of Dante's poem serves not only to compare the experiences of prisoner and pilgrim, but also to suggest their utter incommensurability."[11] Lawrence Langer has articulated that incommensurability as a moment in which high literature and Holocaust testimony are at odds, with no fruitful result possible.[12] Levi overcomes even this tremendous barrier by making that very incongruence a dramatic moment of learning for the reader, as well as a way of emphasizing the bleak reality of the camp.

The miserable irony present in Levi's use of Dante in *Survival in Auschwitz* is representative of his writing strategy as a whole: already brilliant on the surface, but even more dazzling when looked at closely in order to understand the deep connections he makes between the classical traditions he cites and the situation of the Shoah that he describes. The depth of those connections is one focus of this study, and it can only be arrived at through close readings that do not accept the face value of his texts as the only layer of meaning.

Yet risks are incurred through the use of literary strategies. A common view of these risks is espoused by the famed historian Raul Hilberg, in his essay "I Was Not There," as he comments:

> These recreators of the Holocaust, be they historians, sculptors, architects, designers, novelists, playwrights, or poets, are molding something new. They may be shrewd, insightful, or masterful, but they take a larger risk, and all the more so, if they take poetic license to subtract something from the crude reality for the sake of a heightened effect.[13]

It is telling, but not surprising, that Hilberg does include history in this list, but not testimonial writers. Those same risks that he describes can be incurred through testimonial writing that "heightens" its effects in the way that he describes. Levi was more than aware of these potential risks, and he articulates the process of writing and the function of memory as well in order to circumvent as much as possible this perceived threat to the authenticity of his texts.

Chapter 4 further explores Levi's literary strategies, principally the ways in which he transforms autobiography in order to arrive at a collective witnessing and commemoration. The transformation through autobiography to which Foucault alludes takes a radically different form in Levi's work. In the face of the widespread horror of the Shoah, Levi largely shuns the autobiographical genre in favour of a testimony that can represent more than his individual life. Levi's conflation of autobiography into commemoration speaks to the grave burden that post-Holocaust commemorative language must bear. For the victims of the Nazis, there are no individual physical sites of memory, except for memorials designed to represent the masses: no graves, no cemeteries. Brutality towards the victims was extended to their death: the corpses were treated as material traces that had to be obliterated rather than remembered. As Wiesel so eloquently states, "the sky became a common grave" for the victims "whose death numbs the mind."[14]

The Nazis were engaged in a war not only against living victims but also murdered ones: in other words, a war on memory. In the preface to his 1986 volume of essays *The Drowned and the Saved*, Levi quotes Simon Wiesenthal, who recalls the SS telling the prisoners:

> However this war may end, we have won the war against you; none of you will be left to bear witness, but even if someone were to survive, the world would not believe him ... we will destroy the evidence together with you. And even if some proof should remain and some of you survive, people will say that the events you describe are too monstrous to be believed ... We are the ones who will dictate the history of the lagers.[15]

If we take Foucault's dictum seriously in the case of Levi, what emerges is a scenario in which, despite Levi's efforts to contain it as a literary mode, his form of autobiography does achieve a transformation. That transformation is the creation of the writer who can attest to the horror of the Shoah, who can provide cogent witnessing. Yet at the same time he sets this up as an impossible enterprise, through his statements about "true" witnesses all having been killed:

> The story of the Lagers has been written almost exclusively by people who, like me, did not plumb the depths. The ones who did never returned, or if they did their capacity for observation was paralyzed by pain and incomprehension.[16]

The survivor must testify, and yet cannot fully testify, and so Levi's persona as a testimonial writer is put into crisis. The writing persona who must tell the story cannot fulfil that obligation under the strictures that Levi has created. Where does that leave the writing persona itself, always trapped within its own circularity and impossibility? This is a significant conundrum that we encounter in Levi's Holocaust representational lexicon.

To examine Holocaust testimonies is also to involve ourselves in the discourse of shame that stands at the heart of so many of them. In our minds, this shame is an entirely undeserved burden, but nonetheless it must be contended with. The legacy of shame that the Holocaust has left behind, from one circumscribed point of view, can even be said to embody a potentially positive valence, for its examination brings to light aspects of the Nazi inhumanity that bear directly on issues of responsibility and culpability. In other words, the examination of blameless victims points us in an ethical direction: towards the shame of the society that allowed this to happen.

Chapter 5 explores Levi's creation of a theory of the shame he felt and that he believed belonged to the condition of the survivor. Although irrational – Levi clearly states that survivors did not deserve this shame – nonetheless the shame persisted. In order to understand Levi's shame theory as well as his theory of witnessing, we need to examine the ambivalent figure of the *Muselmänner*, those prisoners doubly dehumanized by the camps. As I demonstrate, Levi uses the *Muselmänner* as both a metaphoric figure for shame and a physical representation of that shame.

Levi's shame theory is inextricably entwined with his theory of witnessing and of testimony, and is also deeply related to his autobiographical strategies, as in his lexicon the autobiographical self stands in direct opposition to witnessing. Simply put, in his work the autobiographical self cannot be the self that stands for authoritative witnessing, and so the autobiographical self must be contained in order to make space for witnessing and testimony. As I demonstrate in this book, Levi's theories and practice of witnessing, autobiography, and shame form a vexed nexus of his thought, and his various cultural identities play a strong role in that "natural" philosophy. In often conflicted interrelations between modes of narration and between identities, the brilliance of his work is more fully revealed.

Chapter Two

The Complications of Jewish Identity

Primo Levi's position on his Jewishness has been enigmatic, both for himself and for his readers and critics. During his lifetime, he made differing statements about this identity, ranging from an interview in which he asserted a strong Jewish self to statements that strongly underplay the Jewish part of his identity in favour of the Italian component. In 1975 Levi published an intriguing description of what his Jewish identity meant to him when he was a teenager in the spring of 1938. This passage appears in *The Periodic Table*, the story of his life as a chemist:

> The truth is that until then being Jewish hadn't much mattered to me: privately, and with my Christian friends, I had always considered my origin as a nearly negligible but curious fact, a small, cheerful anomaly, like having a crooked nose or freckles; a Jew is someone who doesn't have a Christmas tree, who shouldn't eat salami but eats it anyway, who learned a little Hebrew at the age of thirteen and then forgot it.[1]

The political scene for Jews in Italy was rapidly shifting in 1938, as the fascist racialist doctrine of the purported impurity of Jews had already become diffuse. The racialist magazine *La difesa della razza* (Defense of the Race), which had as its explicit ideological goal the construction of an "Aryan" race for Christian Italians, would begin publication within a few months, and the July 1938 Manifesto della razza (Race Manifesto) was about to appear, also intended to provide a racialist platform for fascism. The antisemitic Racial Laws would soon follow, in September: first the pseudotheory expressed in the Manifesto and in the journal, and then the very real practice of exclusion and persecution of Italian Jews.[2]

Levi was soon to learn what this exclusion meant, as it became difficult for him to remain at the university. He was only able to begin his chemistry course because of summer exams he had taken: any delay and, like his sister, he would have been forced to wait until after the war to begin his advanced studies. He was under a lot of pressure to succeed at various periodic exams necessary to continue in chemistry.[3] Despite the claims he makes to the contrary, the fact of being Jewish was already significant. Not only Levi but also the entire Jewish community of Turin soon would be suffering under laws eliminating the civil rights of Italian Jews.

Regardless of the politics of exclusion that was rapidly developing, Levi's representation of his Jewish identity has a rather sweet nostalgic tone; he evokes, for example, his bar mitzvah at age thirteen – an event that is a complicated symbol of an often rapid learning of the tradition and, for many Jews, an equally quick forgetting of the same. Yet his description, on the surface a charming and rather innocent recounting of an insignificant difference, has another side to it.

One of the similes that Levi employs to represent the "cheerful anomaly" of Jewishness, the "crooked nose," tells instead a serious story of persecution through imagined physical difference. The figure of the purportedly "Jewish" nose had already been used in antisemitic discourse in Europe for many decades, doing great harm to the image of Jews, and now was being used widely in Fascist anti-Jewish propaganda.[4]

Surprisingly, Levi describes his youthful take on a persecuted Jewish identity in fascist Italy as "cheerful," and as random and potentially "cute" as the revealing nose that was often used as a goad to hatred and derision. His feelings as a young man about the lack of antisemitism in Italy do not seem to have changed with time, even after his experience as a partisan deported to Auschwitz.

The exploration of what Jewish identity meant to Levi during fascism raises important questions that go beyond his individual case: What did it mean to be a Jew in fascist Italy, and how did Levi negotiate an identity that was so strongly Italian with a Jewish identity that made him an outcast? Anti-Jewish campaigns began in the early 1930s with radio broadcasts, newspaper articles, the expulsion of foreign Jews, antisemitic children's novels, and finally the Racial Laws.[5] These laws not only forbade Jewish youth from attending state-run schools and universities, but effectively restricted the professions that Italian Jews could practice, as well as generally prohibiting their hiring non-Jews. The social, economic, and psychological impact on the Jewish community was cruel and devastating. Nonetheless, Levi was asked to give a talk to the Jewish community in Turin in July 1939 on the astounding thesis that antisemitism was at an all-time historical low.[6] That the community could choose this topic as late as 1939 is compelling, and warrants further investigation.

Born in 1919, the year Mussolini's party was formed, Levi was educated within the strictures of fascism, which increasingly sought to achieve national homogeneity. From the early 1930s theories asserting common racial origins of all Christian Italians were propagated; the later Racial Laws were the culmination of the exclusion of Jews from a new, fascist-defined Italian national identity. This generated an identity crisis: where could the civic identity of Italian Jews now reside? How did they negotiate within themselves this painful change in their civic status?

Primo Levi's transformation of life-altering antisemitism into a benign image of a cheerful crooked nose is representative of a set of strategies he adopted to contain or transform a prejudice that ultimately challenges his Italian identity, which he held near and dear. Here it is useful, in order to understand what cultural models were in play for him, to briefly contextualize the concept of Italian Jewish identity.[7] I suggest that Levi's strategies of Jewish self-representation are the direct result of a genealogy of disavowal regarding antisemitism in Italy that began decades before and strongly influenced Levi's generation. Levi's reluctance to acknowledge the life-altering prejudices surrounding him in Fascist Italy is not only a strategy to contain and therefore minimize the bigotry; it is also a marker of a denial whose historical roots lie in myths regarding Jewish emancipation during and after the 1860–61 unification of Italy. In other words, it is not specific to the fascist era. Denial of marginalization was an important part of the narrative regarding the process of integration and acceptance of Italian Jews after unification. Figures such as the nineteenth-century Jewish scientist Cesare Lombroso, who was caught between racially based theories of antisemitism and his own burgeoning field of criminology, and Arnaldo Momigliano, who before the war theorized a smooth and unproblematic post-unification Jewish integration but after the war wrote painful essays about the loss of his family to the Holocaust, demonstrate the distance between the assimilationist goals of the *Risorgimento* and the realities of Jewish life in Italy.[8]

It is my contention that Jews of Levi's generation were strongly influenced by a forcefully optimistic narrative regarding a new secular, specifically Italian Jewish identity that developed between 1860 and the rise of the fascist regime. This left Levi's generation particularly vulnerable to deep feelings of betrayal after antisemitic policies and laws were enacted, as they saw themselves as integral, deeply entrenched members of Italian society, a self-image that was hard for them to entirely abandon despite much evidence that dismantled their previously confident view of their place within Italian society. Levi tellingly discusses the concept of *la patria* in relation to his identity in one of the chapters in *The Drowned and the Saved*: "I myself, in deference to current rhetoric, have declared that I am ready to die for my country. I do not wish to nor can I leave. If I must die, I'll die 'in patria': this will be my way of dying 'for the patria.'"[9]

This context helps us to better situate the contradictions and complications of Levi's representation of Jewishness both for himself and for others. How Levi's differing positions on his Jewish identity interact, and what they convey about Italian Jewish identity, are significant. Not only does his Jewish self-representation speak to his own complex identity, but it also reflects a post-Holocaust crisis of identity that is quite specific to the situation of Italian Jews.[10]

Levi had several components to who he was, as he was Italian, a chemist, a writer, Jewish, and a Holocaust survivor. Of these, his Jewishness was the most problematic, both in his relation to it and in how it was imposed by the outside world. Berel Lang, in considering a possible definition of Jewish identity, writes:

> Put more exactly, the question would ask, "What *are* Jewish identity?" – the grammatical implausibility reflecting the incongruous assembly subsumed under a single rubric. Here religion and culture, history and politics, psychology and morality, faith and common sense elbow each other for place, each of them confident of its own claims but vague or even indifferent about what is due the others.[11]

What might appear as contradictions in Levi's situation can also be read as components of the list that Lang elaborates. Why Levi's Jewishness is the most overdetermined of his various identities has much to do with choice and with imposition. It is, after all, one he did not choose, from this respect radically dissimilar from his scientific and writerly identities. Lang also remarks that "reference to personal identity, whatever else it entails, addresses the character of the self – not only its identification by others but its own self-definition."[12]

As the philosopher Sidney Hook says about Jewish definition:

Some people ask, What makes you a Jew? I say, a Jew is anyone who calls himself such or is called such and lives in a community which acts on the distinction between Jew and non-Jew. That's a purely nominal definition, but it's the only one that does justice to the way the term "Jew" is used throughout the world.[13]

The tension apparent in Hook's statement between the person that calls himself a Jew and the person who is called a Jew is particularly relevant to Levi's situation. When Levi's partisan band was caught by the Fascist militia in December 1943, he ran a calculated risk: he admitted to being Jewish rather than a partisan because he believed that partisans would be executed immediately. But instead the Fascists turned him over to the Germans as a Jew. That his community "acted upon the distinction" was a defining moment for Levi, as he was deported to Auschwitz as a Jew and not as an Italian partisan.

Several other factors must be taken into account before the complex situation of Levi's Jewishness can be even partially understood. How Levi himself experienced this identity, how he chose to present it to the world, how the outside world viewed him, and, finally, the relation of his Judaism to other of his key identity components are all crucial elements. Previous analyses of Levi's Jewish identity have centred primarily on three main aspects. The first is what I call the implementation of his Jewish identity: whether he and his family practised Judaism, and what various levels of practice might say about convictions regarding Judaism and its importance to him. The second is how and what he says about Jews and Judaism in relation to the subject matter of his writings. The third is what he says about his own Jewish identity in interviews and essays.[14]

There is, however, a fourth aspect to this subject, much less studied, which is how he represents Jewish identity – both his own identity and that of others – figurally in his imaginative and testimonial works. This aspect is a principal focus below, although in order to contextualize the meaning of his representations of Jewishness, other components are also discussed.

Assimilation and Identity

One of the first issues I will raise concerns Levi's Jewish practice as well as its public perception. The misnomer "assimilated Jew" has frequently

been applied to Levi, often because his immediate family was not Orthodox, which is the type of Judaism officially practised in Italy. In the
strength of their identification with Jewish culture and religious practices, however, Levi's family was typical of many Italian Jewish families
at the time: closer to the practice of Conservative or Reform Judaism in
the United States or Britain, even though in Italy those forms of Judaism
did not formally exist.[15] The biographical record of Levi's involvement
with institutional Judaism speaks for itself, as Levi had a bar mitzvah at
the traditional age of thirteen, which involved two years of intense religious preparation for the event. His immediate family observed major
holidays and had strong ties with his mother's more religious side of
the family, who were still for the most part practising Jews whose connection to the previous generations' Orthodoxy was strong.

Levi was also subject to harassment as a school child in part because
he was Jewish.[16] Given his family's practices, it is obvious that Levi's
family had a distinct Jewish identity, albeit not an Orthodox one. In
The Periodic Table and elsewhere, Levi recounts how his father loved
prosciutto and would buy and consume it while out of the house as a
guilty pleasure. This spirit of mutiny against the laws of *kashrut* that
forbid the eating of pork can be interpreted as a sign of secular Judaism,
signalling as it does a simultaneous recognition of and rebellion against
religious practice. It is not in itself a mark of assimilation: moments like
these indicate instead the stalwart and strong presence of a culture to be
rebelled against and reformulated rather than abandoned. The inaccurate term "assimilated Jew" has in Levi's case caused much confusion
and has shed no light on his actual cultural identity.

The problem of the term "assimilated Jew" goes well beyond the
case of Levi. "Assimilation," from the Latin *assimilatio*, to render similar, has been widely misused to indicate the fate of a minor culture as
it encounters and negotiates the exigencies of coexisting with a dominant culture. The term is broadly used rather than the more accurate
terms "integration" or "acculturation." The implication of "assimilation," found in the Latin root, is an abandonment of the original culture in favour of the new. During and after the Enlightenment, Jewish
assimilation was a major topic of debate both for Jewish communities
and for Christian cultural figures that were interested in Jewish intellectual ideas.[17] The elimination of visible difference seemed to be the only
viable path to achieving tolerance if not acceptance. The very fact of the
mislabelling points to a serious underlying concern, that Christian society often resists the notion that culturally or philosophically identified
Jews could still be Jews.[18]

This issue lies at the heart of any discussion of Levi's Jewish identity: if the differences between "assimilated" and "secular" Judaism are not understood, then Levi's Jewish identity is bound to be misunderstood or worse. The label "assimilated Jew" indeed turns the religious and cultural identity of that individual into fair game for cultural hegemony. One of Levi's biographers, for example, sees no obstacle in perceiving him as "assimilated." Evidently this led him to presume that Levi celebrated Christian holidays (which he did not): the biographer comments at one point, without apparent irony, that "the Levis endured a joyless Christmas."[19] Bryan Cheyette has remarked on the appropriation of Primo Levi within what he calls the "Christianized discourses of forgiveness and redemption," against which Levi rebelled several times, but that have nonetheless persisted.[20]

Looking closely at the specifically Jewish history of Levi and his family helps to contextualize not only how he was viewed by the outside world but also his own representation of his Jewishness. Levi's family had moved to Turin from the Piedmontese countryside only a generation before, leaving the small town of Bene Vagienna, where they had encountered overt discrimination. The two dominant institutions exemplifying and actively promoting cultural hegemony in this period of Italian history, fascism and Catholicism, became linked after the Lateran Pact of 1929. As the years of fascism wore on, more and more attempts were made to achieve national homogeneity. Theories expounding the common racial origins of all Christian Italians were propagated.[21] These claims excluded from *italianità* an entire generation of patriotic Italian Jews, many of whom had fought in World War I and swore such a strong allegiance to Italian royalty that they often named their sons and daughters after the king and queen. The Racial Laws of 1938–39 were the culmination of this exclusion.[22]

When Levi was seventeen years old, Mussolini stepped up the racialist campaign that was already being promoted in Italy. In early 1938, he published the Manifesto della razza (Race Manifesto), a document that claimed racial unity for Italians but excluded Jews. For several years previously, an antisemitic campaign had been launched in the form of newspaper articles, antisemitic children's books, and a magazine entitled *La difesa della razza* (Defence of the Race), which proposed theories of racial inferiority and superiority. Mussolini also quietly moved to exclude Jews from positions of power all over Italy beginning as early as 1930.[23]

The Racial Laws of 1938 and 1939 prohibited Jewish students from attending public schools, but Levi, as mentioned above, managed to finish his degree at the university, although not without some problems due to these restrictions. Around this time he became involved in the local Jewish community in Turin: he attended a study group for two years during which he became engrossed in Jewish intellectual culture.

After graduating the university, Levi looked for jobs in his field, which was difficult because of his Jewishness. When the Germans invaded Italy in September 1943, Levi joined a partisan band that had been infiltrated by a fascist spy. Captured, persecuted as a Jew, and deported to Auschwitz, he became a slave labourer for IG Farben. Levi returned to Italy in 1946, after a long circuitous journey home. He immediately sought a publisher for his testimony, *If This Is a Man*, and finally found a small publisher willing to take on what was considered an unpopular topic. His writing career continued in the postwar period with the publication of essays, poetry, and short stories.

At this point in his life, a persecuted Jewish identity had been stamped upon him from the outside, a process that began with the Racial Laws. When he became an internationally recognized Holocaust writer, his identity as a survivor and as a Holocaust writer also became indelibly marked upon him. Levi felt that bearing witness and testifying through his work was a crucial mission, both for his own need to re-establish himself as an individual after being treated as less than human by the Nazis, and for educational purposes. He embraced the role of Holocaust educator, visiting schools, meeting children, and describing his experiences to them. At the same time he tried to establish his career as a writer whose topics were not limited to the Holocaust. The tensions between different components of his identity became apparent at this time. Known almost exclusively as a Holocaust writer and survivor, Levi for much of his career had to struggle to get himself seen in any other light.

In the 1960s, he became interested in exploring Yiddish and Ashkenazi language and literature. This eastern European Jewish tradition is not prevalent in Italy, which is dominated by Sephardic (of Spanish origin) Jewish culture. Levi wanted to familiarize himself with the predominant Jewish culture that was largely destroyed by the Holocaust, in order to better understand the lives of eastern Europeans Jews. This research culminated in the 1982 publication of his Jewish partisan novel *If Not Now, When?* One critic interestingly remarks that "Levi's post-Holocaust writing represents a meeting between his 'native' Italian, Western culture and the 'foreign' Jewish culture that he tried to make his own after Auschwitz," yet incorrectly postulates that Levi knew nothing about the Hebrew tradition before this time, ignoring the fact of his bar mitzvah.[24]

Levi became ensnarled in debates about Israel and Palestine in the 1980s, in which he tried to clarify the distinction between Jews and Zionists, pleasing neither the left in Italy nor supporters of Israel. In an interview with Edith Bruck, he says that he is incapable of an objective judgment on Israel; that the Israel supported by the right is precisely that aspect of Israel that he likes the least.[25] After the Israeli invasion of Lebanon in 1982, Levi, along with many others, called for Prime Minister Begin's resignation. He remarks, in a 1983 interview with Giampaolo Pansa, that "because I am certain that Israel must be defended, I believe in the painful necessity of an efficient army. But I am equally sure that it would do the Israeli government good to deal with support from us which is never unconditional."[26] He was roundly attacked for such views, accused of being anti-Israel, although this was far from the truth. As both a Jew and a well-known Holocaust survivor, Levi was expected to support Israel uncritically. His opinions on the matter, however well thought out, were sometimes interpreted as a lack of loyalty to his Jewish identity. Cheyette comments that Levi's stance regarding Israel, although perceived incorrectly, even affected his ability to publish in the United States.[27] That stance is rehearsed even today as a form of critique of Zionism, cited out of context and without regard to Levi's comments quoted above.[28]

Levi complained that for American audiences, his Jewish identity was the most important aspect of him, and for Italian audiences, it was underplayed. His Jewish identity was alternatively highlighted and pigeonholed inseparably from his identity as a Holocaust survivor, both of which were constituted in part by racialist policies in Fascist Italy. Levi's new postwar self included an overdetermined Jewish identity, foisted upon him by persecution, that stands apart from the Jewish identity he acquired from his family. His postwar identity is multifaceted: he is a chemist and a writer, a dual identity he develops in his writings; a Holocaust survivor persecuted because he was Jewish – and one who survived Auschwitz because he self-identified as a chemist and therefore lived through the second brutal Polish winter by obtaining work in the laboratory.

Levi was interested in thematizing his identity as a scientist and as a writer in some of his essays and interviews, and does so in interesting and thoughtful ways, even comparing the process of writing to chemical combinations and processes.[29] He does not, however, often engage the subject of his Jewish identity except in a very limited fashion. He describes it in one of the following three ways, most often as a result of being asked about it: he either relegates it to the effects of persecution, indicates his level of interest in Jewish culture, or quantifies how Jewish he felt in opposition to how Italian he felt, as if the two identity formations constituted a binary opposition.

Another important aspect of Levi's Jewish identity is the relationship of this identity to persecution. The ways in which he articulates the issue of oppression are complex and multifaceted, and reveal strategies for negotiating a difficult identity in the face of fascist and Nazi persecution. Massimo Giuliani has commented that "it was Auschwitz (since the racial laws of 1938) that molded his Jewish identity and matured the specific character of Italian Jewishness in him."[30] This characterization, accurate in many respects, does not take into account Levi's own resistance to labelling and how he perceived his own identity. The identity of persecution in Levi's case is complicated by the fact of the persecution itself. How his Jewish identity might have played out in other circumstances is a point of speculation for Levi himself, evident in his remarks about it.

There is a clear danger, however, in an approach that views Levi's identity solely as a result of persecution, despite his own comments on this. As Sergio Parussa has noted, "even though Primo Levi's notion of Jewish identity intertwines with his writing ... and both are linked to the experience of the Shoah, drawing a straight line between them could lead to dangerous simplifications."[31] Parussa's point is that what we are dealing with is more than the sum of its parts and should not be reduced to a formulaic view of Levi's writing and his identity as an uncomplicated effect of persecution.

Levi's own attitudes towards this part of his identity demonstrate a certain resistance to his Jewishness, apparent in the sometimes contradictory statements he has made about it. The overdetermination of Jewish identity may be precisely what Levi is rebelling against. Levi's comments about his Jewish identity are mostly to be found in interviews, where he was asked questions about it over and over, perhaps quite tediously for him. In one interview he states:

I became a Jew in Auschwitz. Before Auschwitz, I did not feel like a Jew. The awareness of being different was forced upon me ... Auschwitz gave me something new. It made me become a Jew, and so I discovered a cultural heritage that I did not have earlier.[32]

What Levi means by "becoming a Jew" becomes clearer when we look at a telling remark he made about Ashkenazi Jews: "when I came into contact with them, I discovered with surprise that they were full-time Jews, while I was only *un ebreo anagrafico*" – a Jew registered with the Jewish community of Turin, as he clarifies elsewhere.[33] Does this signify that Levi felt Italian Jewishness in its acculturated state did not count for much when confronted with the "full-time" Jewishness of the Ashkenazi Jews he met in Auschwitz, or is it another attempt to minimize his Italian Jewish identity?

Levi's statements regarding his Jewish identity are at times inconsistent. In an interview with Giuseppe Grieco, he makes it clear that he had a religious upbringing and that he has a Jewish identity that he has "no intention of discarding." Elsewhere he relegates Jewish identity to a very small bit of his overall identity and does not acknowledge the strength of his religious education.[34] In a 1976 interview entitled "Jewish, Up to a Point," Edith Bruck asks Levi what it means to him to be Jewish. Levi replies, "I was turned into a Jew by others. Before Hitler I was a middle-class Italian boy. The experience of the Race Laws helped me to recognize, amongst the many threads that made up the Jewish tradition, a number that I could accept." He elaborates that spiritual independence and the Talmudic tradition of "impassioned but precise argument" are parts of the Jewish legacy that he has adopted. But when asked about antisemitism, Levi replied that even during fascism, antisemitism was "never more than superficial and inconsistent."[35] This puzzling answer sidesteps the historical fact that antisemitism in Italy during the fascist era was widespread and cruel. His self-representation embraces some contradictory moments, as evidenced by these varying statements, and the meaning of these contradictions goes beyond that of inconsistency.

The pressure of his Jewish identity was intense. If he criticized a policy or action of the Israeli government, he was in turn criticized for being "anti-Israel"; if he was understood to be Jewish, then he was expected to conform to certain expectations of a Jew; if he was described as "assimilated," then his Judaism was taken away from him completely. For many years, his writings were categorized as "only" survivor testimony and therefore of interest by and large only to Jews; he was considered to be out of the mainstream of Italian literary culture because of his Jewishness and because of his survivor identity, despite his assertions of being an Italian first.[36] During this period, his writings on other subjects were not taken as seriously as his Holocaust writings.

When Levi's true qualities as a writer's writer finally became obvious to critics, the ensuing tendency was to talk about him as an Italian writer, claim him as a native son, and marginalize the Jewish aspects of his work.

In sum, the paradoxes that emerge in Levi's Jewish identity are indicative of the confusion surrounding what is perceived as Jewish by the outside world, compounded by Levi's own often contradictory positions on the subject. His own statements do not always shed much light on the issue, as they are not only contradictory but are fraught with tensions regarding the proper definition of a Jew. Critics wanting to peg him as a Jewish writer or as a writer seen solely within a persecutory mode have wittingly or unwittingly also played into this conundrum.

Literary Representations of Jewishness

A literary approach to the question of Levi's Jewish identity is perhaps the riskiest of all, if what is sought is an empirical, quantitative understanding of Levi's Jewish identity. Looking at his representational strategies for Judaism and Jewishness, however, provides the most fruitful and nuanced results regarding the complexity of his thought about Jewishness and his own place within it.

There are several vital moments in which Levi thematizes Jewish identity in ways that go well beyond the problematic and misleading binary opposition of Italian versus Jewish, and they extend beyond the concept of a persecuted identity as well. The first of these moments is found in the poem at the beginning of *Survival in Auschwitz* entitled "Shemà," published in 1947.[37]

"Shemà" appears as an epigraph, thereby setting the tone for the testimony to follow:

Voi che vivete sicuri
Nelle vostre tiepede case
Voi che trovate tornando a sera
Il cibo caldo e visi amici
    Considerate se questo è un uomo
    Che lavora nel fango
    Che non conosce pace
    Che lotta per mezzo pane
    Che muore per un sì o per un no
    Considerate se questa è una donna

Senza capelli e senza nome
Senza più forza di ricordare
Vuoti gli occhi e freddo il grembo
Come una rana d'inverno
Meditate che questo è stato
Vi commando queste parole
Scolpitele nel vostro cuore
Stando in casa andando per via
Coricandovi alzandovi;
Ripetetele ai vostri figli.
O vi si sfaccia la casa
La malattia vi impedisca
I vostri nati torcano il viso da voi

You who live safe
In your warm houses
You who find, returning in the evening,
Hot food and friendly faces:
Consider if this is a man
Who works in the mud
Who does not know peace
Who fights for a little bread
Who dies for a yes or a no.
Consider if this is a woman,
Without hair and without name
With no more strength to remember,
Her eyes empty and her womb cold
Like a frog in winter.
Meditate that this happened:
I command these words to you.
Carve them in your hearts
At home, in the street,
Going to bed, getting up:
Repeat them to your children,
Or may your house fall apart,
May illness impede you,
May your children turn their faces from you.[38]

Parussa has called this poem a kind of "negative theology,"[39] but it goes far beyond that in scope, as Levi intensely negotiates his Jewish identity and the issue of secularization in this poem that is so indebted

to the Jewish liturgical tradition. The title of the poem is taken from the
name of the central prayer in Judaism, which is a call to monotheism
and also a call to Jews to remember who they are and who their God is.
The name of the prayer, *Sh'ma*, means "to listen":

> Hear, O Israel, the Lord is our God, the Lord is One.
> Blessed be the name of the glory of His kingdom forever and ever.
> You shall love the Lord your God with all your heart, with all your
> soul and with all your might. And these words that I command you
> today shall be upon your heart. You shall teach them thoroughly
> to your children, and you shall speak of them when you sit in your
> house and when you walk on the road, when you lie down and
> when you rise. You shall bind them as a sign upon your hand, and
> they shall be for a reminder between your eyes. And you shall write
> them upon the doorposts of your house and upon your gates.[40]

There are evident correlations between Levi's poem "Shemà" and the
first section of the original *Sh'ma*, known as the *V'hafta*: Levi echoes
the command to bind the words upon the body, to inscribe them on
the doorposts and gates with his injunction to carve the words in the
heart and to repeat them to the children. These injunctions begin with
the title of the poem, with the commandment to listen, and therefore to
remember.

The adaptation, appropriation even, of part of the *Sh'ma* as a call for
Holocaust memory raises compelling issues. The "I" of Levi's poem,
in "I command these words to you," evokes the question of the position that Levi puts himself in by adapting the prayer in this way. In
more than a secular rewriting, the survivor, who invokes his readers
to remember and then to tell their children, places himself in the position of an ultimate authority. And that authority emphasizes as well the
dangers of forgetting:

> Or may your house fall apart,
> May illness impede you,
> May your children turn their faces from you.

This also constitutes a rewriting of the end of the second passage of
the *Sh'ma*:

> Take care lest your heart be lured away, and you turn astray and worship
> alien gods and bow down to them. For then the Lord's wrath will flare up

against you, and He will close the heavens so that there will be no rain and the earth will not yield its produce, and you will swiftly perish from the good land which the Lord gives you.

In Levi's secular "Shemà," the writing that memorializes the Holocaust must become part of Jewish memory, in order to make sure that future generations know what happened. As Parussa thoughtfully comments, "by means of a secular and rational resumption of Jewish religious themes, through their reactualization, Levi contributes to the reconstruction of Jewish cultural memory."[41] But writing alone is not sufficient to ensure this: Levi goes well beyond the injunction of the inscribing found in the *Sh'ma* with his command to carve the words in our hearts. The role that Levi as survivor and as writer embraces is to command rather than commend remembrance, through this evocative rewriting of the most central prayer in the Jewish tradition.[42]

His poem's last line also speaks to this imperative. If you don't listen and pass along the tradition of remembering, then may your children turn their faces from you. May the next generation not recognize the last, leading to the abolition of generational continuity and therefore history if this particular and critical history is not remembered. If you do not teach these words to your children, then may history cease to be. This poem represents some of Levi's most unveiled sentiments regarding the urgency of Holocaust writing and remembrance. Levi's last line connects his use of the prayer in the poem to his project of exploring the ramifications of dehumanization. The commemoration of the Shoah is presented as a post-Holocaust necessity. Just as the poem appropriates the position of a higher authority in the service of commemoration, here too the relevance of a higher authority in this dehumanized context is raised. Levi, in his role as the bearer of the memory of the atrocity, might as well be God remembering the world.

The issue of secularization is subsumed into the command for Holocaust remembrance as the imperative shifts from the monotheistic enterprise of traditional Judaism to the urgency of a commemorative mode. This outcome is emblematic of Levi's subject position vis-á-vis Judaism as well as the persecution that so deeply marked him as a Jew. His knowledge of Jewish tradition allows him to integrate that same tradition with a secular reinscribing. The date of composition of this poem is also noteworthy. Written right after the war, as Levi was immersed in thoughts of memory and testimony and how best to express them, the poem can be seen as a negotiation between what happened to Levi as a Jew during the Holocaust and his understanding of his Jewish identity, past and present. The tortured status of that identity, foisted at least in part upon him, is reflected in the tone of the poem.

There are two other textual moments in *Survival in Auschwitz* that address the question of Levi's attitude towards religion and the position of God, as well as towards the question of a reformulation of Jewish identity. The first is found in his horrified recounting of a selection in the camp, one that ends with a bunkmate of his condemned to death and another expressing his thanks at not being selected:

A poco a poco prevale il silenzio, e allora, dalla mia cuccetta che è al terzo piano, si vede e si sente che il vecchio Kuhn prega, ad alta voce. Col berretto in testa e dodolando il busto con violenza, Kuhn ringrazia Dio perché non è stato scelto.

Kuhn è un insensato. Non vede, nella cuccetta accanto, Beppe il Greco che ha vent'anni, e dopodomani andrà in gas, e lo sa, e se ne sta sdraiato e guarda fissa la lampadina senza dire niente e senza più pensare niente? Non sa Kuhn che la prossima volta sarà la sua volta? Non capisce Kuhn che è accaduto oggi un abominio che nessuna preghiera propiziatoria, nessun perdono, nessuna espiazione dei colpevoli, nulla insomma che sia in potere dell'uomo di fare, potrà risanare mai più?

Se io fossi Dio, sputerei a terra la preghiera di Kuhn.[43]

Silence slowly prevails, and then, from my bunk, on the top level, I see and hear old Kuhn praying aloud, with his cap on his head, his torso swaying violently. Kuhn is thanking God that he was not chosen. Kuhn is out of his mind. Does he not see, in the bunk next to him, Beppo the Greek, who is twenty years old and is going to the gas chamber the day after tomorrow, and knows it, and lies there staring at the light without saying anything and without even thinking anymore? Does Kuhn not know that next time it will be his turn? Does Kuhn not understand that what happened today is an abomination, which no propitiatory prayer, no pardon, no expiation by the guilty – nothing at all in the power of man to do – can ever heal? If I were God, I would spit Kuhn's prayer out upon the ground.[44]

The intensity of this passage is striking, not only for Levi's dramatic pronouncement at the end but for several other aspects. The visibility of Kuhn's Jewish practice intrudes upon the tense silence after the selection. Kuhn's praying is both heard and seen, as he prays in the traditional Jewish manner of *davening*, bowing back and forth. His praying aloud is a traditional and usual means of prayer.

Levi's narrative perspective stands outside of this common prayer tradition, as if he himself was unfamiliar with it, describing Kuhn's actions perhaps for the reader presumed to be ignorant of the manner and style of Jewish prayer. His outrage at Kuhn's insensitivity appears to be directed at the visual and aural aspects of Kuhn's behaviour: praying publicly, loudly, in such a manner that is noticeable by all. Yet what appears to be an attack on Orthodox prayer practice – a practice Levi would have seen in the Turin synagogue many times growing up – is better understood as an attack on the insensitivity of the individual who ignores the dehumanization of the camp, the changed moral code that affects all the prisoners. Levi's description conveys a strong discomfort with the prayer practice in the context of the camp.

Kuhn's actions are directly compared to those of his fellow prisoner, Beppo, condemned to death and no longer able to think or act like a man. Levi's title for his testimony, *If This Is a Man*, comes to mind vividly when this passage is read. The contrast is striking, as the reader is presented with two extremes: Kuhn, insensitive, praying to a God that Levi believes would spit at a prayer that does not acknowledge the damage done to humankind, to the world, by the exterminations, and that does not see beyond one individual's fate; and Beppo, dehumanization taken to its extreme, when the condemned does not even appear to react to his own impending death. The loss of thought that Beppo embodies signals the end of what is human to Levi. He frequently thematizes this crisis of humanity in his testimony, primarily through the figure of the *Musselmänner* that I discuss in chapter 5.

Later on, Levi declares, "Today I think that if only because an Auschwitz existed no one in our age should speak of Providence."[45] Tellingly, these words appear at the end of his testimony, with the dissolution of the camp in sight. Levi's last chapter, "The Story of Ten Days," recounts the period of time after the departure of the Nazis, when critically ill prisoners were left on their own with no resources, illness and death all around them. In this part of the chapter, a liminal space is created in which freedom appears as a possibility, but is still elusive. The concept of Providence, especially where the term is capitalized, is generally taken to mean God's intervention in the world, the notion of God as an actor in history. These lines reflect the content of Levi's scepticism regarding God as that being who could have prevented the genocide: the God to whom and for whom it makes no sense to pray. The "stories of a new Bible" that Levi calls for earlier in the text constitute a reformulation of Jewish identity conceptualized without a traditional notion of God.

Levi's hypothetical clause at the end of the Kuhn episode – "If I were God" – is a vivid reminder of his subject position in "Shemà." It suggests as well another moment in Levi's opus in which a religious paradigm is used, this time to evoke the power of science. Later in his writing career, in *The Periodic Table*, Levi recounts an illicit chemical experiment embarked upon when he was still in *liceo*, with his friend Enrico, whose brother had a chemistry laboratory. After breaking into the lab to conduct some experiments, Levi declares his feelings about this new scientific adventure:

> Per me, la chimica rappresentava una nuvola indefinita di potenze future, che avvolgeva il mio avvenire in nere volute lacerate da bagliori di fuoco, simile e quella che occultava il monte Sinai. Come Mosè, da quella nuvola attendevo la mia legge, l'ordine in me, attorno a me e nel mondo.[46]

> For me chemistry represented a vague cloud of imminent powers, which enveloped my future in black spirals torn by flashes of fire, like the one that obscured Mount Sinai. Like Moses, I expected from that cloud my law, order in myself, around me, and in the world.[47]

Levi was fifteen years old when he became interested in chemistry, and he uses striking metaphors to describe what science means to him. One can surmise that at this stage of his life, two years after his bar mitzvah, he has found a substitute for religion in science and its greater potential for answering his questions and explaining the universe.

Imaginative Recastings of Identity: *The Periodic Table*

Elsewhere in *The Periodic Table*, there are explorations of Jewish identity that are formulated in significantly different ways than what is found in *Survival in Auschwitz*. The first chapter, "Argon," published some thirty years after the poem "Shemà," reveals an imaginative recasting of what Jewish experience in Italy was in his family and for himself. *The Periodic Table* is not primarily testimonial, and is generally more literary in its emphasis on storytelling rather than on accurate detail. It reflects as well Levi's desire to try out different literary genres, and ultimately to challenge what genre can mean in relation to history and fictive retellings of history.

"Argon" depends on a fictive mode and embellished, handed-down stories. Alberto Cavaglion has even called Levi's narrative strategy in this chapter "dissimulation" as a way of underscoring the fact that the details given, as precise as they may seem on the surface, simply cannot be trusted as a source of truth or certainty, as much as the reader or biographer may want to believe them. "In Argon imagination reigns over truth," Cavaglion argues. "The biographers have ransacked the story, and the articles connected with the story, wrongly believing them to be a precious source through which to 'read' Levi's life. Nothing is more mistaken."[48] It is in the interstices between fiction and a historical mode that Levi's most interesting ideas about identity and culture are to be found. A close look at "Argon" is warranted not only because it is the first chapter of *The Periodic Table*, but because it reflects how Levi wants to tell the story of his own life, and because it sets up Levi's modus operandi for the entire text. The approach that Levi develops will culminate in the last chapter, "Carbon," which is the most theoretically adventuresome section of the book.

At a glance, the chapter might seem to be an anomaly, an odd way of opening *The Periodic Table*: the tale is, after all, mostly about his idiosyncratic ancestors, and the tone as well as the topic differ markedly from those in the chapters that follow. These tales in "Argon," however, reveal the strategies of integration adopted by those characters he calls his ancestors, and thus are important thematically for Levi's sense of Jewishness and what that means. His family had recently moved to Turin from the Piemontese countryside and so the chapter focuses mainly on the Jewish community of the rural areas of Piedmont. Using "argon" as a rich and complex metaphor, Levi's tale is charged with ambivalences regarding cultural integration. The themes he explores in this opening chapter to *The Periodic Table*, ostensibly the story of his life as a chemist, are very relevant to a theory of history that reveals his understanding of the Piedmontese Jewish community and his own place within it.

The chapter also explores a narrative voice that subsumes questions of personal identity and autobiography into the story of the community. As Massimo Giuliani asserts, "this is the true and the most authentic Jewish background of Levi's personality ... [these pages] constitute that cultural, daily Judaism that is, without solution of continuity, Levi's Jewish identity."[49] Giuliani's reading is dependent on taking

Levi's stories at face value, rather than taking into account the fictional element that is present. Yet the ways in which Cavaglion's assertions about "Argon" (that it is largely fictional) and Giuliani's (that it constitutes Levi's cultural Judaism) intersect are intriguing, and do not necessarily constitute binary oppositions or contradictions, as much as contradictions may seem likely. Levi's own narrative strategy in "Argon" will make clear why a binary opposition is not useful in considering this chapter, as this strategy involves a delicate weaving of truth and fiction in order to arrive at his narrative goals. Levi is giving us the construction of a Jewish identity that is ultimately grounded in the writer's imagination.

"Argon" begins with a discourse on the nature of inert gases, including argon:

> In the air we breathe are the so-called inert gases. They bear curious Greek names of scholarly origin, which signify "the New," "the Hidden," "the Lazy," "the Foreigner." In fact, they are so inert, so satisfied with their condition, that they don't interfere in any chemical reaction or combine with any other element, and so they passed unobserved for centuries.[50]

Having adopted this striking language of self-satisfied inertness, Levi then makes a direct comparison between these gases and his ancestors:

> From the little I know of my forebears they resemble these gases. They were not all physically inert, because that was not granted to them: rather, they were, or had to be, fairly active, in order to earn a living and because of a dominant morality according to which "if you don't work you don't eat"; but inert they undoubtedly were deep down, inclined to disinterested speculation, witty conversation, elegant, pedantic, and gratuitous argument. It can't be coincidence if the activities attributed to them, while extremely varied, have in common something static, an attitude of dignified abstention, of voluntary (or accepted) relegation to the margin of the great river of life. Noble, inert, and rare.[51]

A certain ambivalence mixed with pride characterizes this chapter, as he recounts the history of the ancestors' immigration to Italy in around 1500, describing their difficulties in settling into the region:

> Rejected, or not warmly welcomed, in Turin, they settled in various agricultural towns in southern Piedmont, where they introduced the

technology of silk; even in the most prosperous periods, they were never more than an extremely small minority. They were neither much loved nor much hated; no stories of notable persecutions have been handed down, yet a wall of suspicion, of undefined hostility, of scorn, must have kept them essentially separate from the rest of the population until many decades after the emancipation of 1848 ... As always happens, the rejection was mutual.[52]

Levi raises the notion of integration in provocative ways, as he makes clear that any blending with the local population was not a goal for this generation of Jews. The nervous cohabitation of the two cultures he describes is characterized instead by secrecy and tension. Levi's ambivalence about integration and what it means is apparent in the very choice of metaphor for this episode. *Argon* is chosen as the element to which he compares his relatives: and argon, as he tells us, does not interfere – but it also does not combine well.

Levi's comparison of his ancestors to noble gases contrasts the invisibility of those gases with Jewish visibility, ultimately addressing the vulnerability of the Jews. Readers are drawn to imagine how different the history of Jewish persecution would be if Jewish communities were not perceived as presenting the threat of combining or interfering with other cultures, and so could go undetected and therefore unmolested. In the post-Holocaust context in which Levi writes, this comparison between the qualities of argon and his ancestors is particularly compelling. It projects a longed-for inconspicuousness that is precisely the opposite of what Levi describes in his recounting of his ancestors' tense relations with the gentile community.

How precisely does argon work as a metaphor for these ancestors? Levi creates a paranomastic tension in the very choice of argon from the other noble gases he lists. The situation of *argon* in the case of these Jewish settlers in Piedmont is closer to *agon*, and perhaps is meant to suggest it, as they struggle with their environment, new culture and new neighbours, creating a linguistic shield along the way that he describes as both protective and aggressive: a tension between the Greek term *agon*, that references struggle or contest, and *argon*, also Greek, meaning inert, or literally without work.

In his analysis of the rapport between the two cultures in this opening chapter, Levi looks at the interaction of the two languages, Piedmontese dialect and Hebrew, that resulted in the development of a jargon specific to the region. He discusses this jargon as a linguistic accommodation that expresses both the richness and the difficulty of this cultural standoff:

> It has a marvelous comic force, arising from the contrast between the fabric of the speech, which is the rough, sober, and laconic Piedmontese dialect, never written except on a bet, and the Hebrew framework, plucked from the remote language of the fathers ... But this contrast mirrors another, that essential conflict of the Jews of the Diaspora, scattered among "the peoples" (the *gôjím*, that is), and stretched between divine vocation and the daily misery of exile.[53]

The culture that these ancestors bring with them is not easily subsumed or abandoned; in fact, one of the more fascinating aspects of this chapter is the description of the inventive and resistant ways in which they negotiate the new culture around them. This is particularly noteworthy in the development of new vocabulary to describe Christian culture:

> The original, Hebrew form is much more profoundly corrupted, and for two reasons: in the first place, secrecy was strictly necessary, because comprehension of such words on the part of Gentiles could have led to the dangerous accusation of sacrilege; in the second place, the mangling had the precise purpose of denying, of obliterating, the magical-sacred content of the word, hence eliminating any supernatural quality ... Completely – and predictably – cryptic and indecipherable is the term "Odò," which one used, when it really couldn't be helped, to refer to Christ, lowering one's voice and looking around circumspectly: it's as well to mention Christ as infrequently as possible, because the myth of the Deicide People dies hard.[54]

Levi references the history of Jewish persecution through this fascinating linguistic accommodation. His brilliant cultural analysis reveals the mechanisms of the renaming that simultaneously removes content and creates solidarity through a secret language for Christianity.

In order to understand Levi's concept of history in this chapter, and its relation to Jewish identity, it is important to look more carefully at what he means by "ancestor." Are these characters actually related to him? Levi, after generically calling them *antenati*, refers to specific ones as "aunt" or "uncle":

> As for the term "uncle," I should point out immediately that it has to be understood in a very broad sense. It's customary among us to call "uncle"

any old relative, however distant; and since all or almost all the old people of the community are, ultimately, our relatives, it follows that we have a large number of uncles.[55]

The other way to look at this situation is to understand that the number of actual uncles was very small. Levi is evoking a genealogical slippery slope, as he claims as an ancestor almost any old Jewish person in the area, thus disclaiming the need for an actual blood relation for his ancestry. Levi's genea-logic moves from "all or almost all" to "ultimately," *alla lunga*, in the long run, in the original Italian. We have to wonder, however, for just how long we are expected to go: after all, the period he is describing is more than four hundred years. Does an uncle remain an uncle within that time frame, given all the possible genealogical permutations? Or is the use of the term "uncle" – and by association this fantastical genealogy – instead a rhetorical strategy, and if so how does it work?

The imaginary genealogy of the first part of the chapter melds into his actual genealogy, as the chapter ends with an anecdote about his paternal grandmother, an episode in which Levi as a child appears. Levi's entertaining narration provides the space in which this long jump from the history of a community to specific and actual relatives can emerge seamlessly, according to the rhetorical terms of his narration, but there is much imbedded behind that desired seamlessness. A fictive, rather than historical, mode is the bedrock upon which this story is built, underscored by the oral tradition that Levi tells us has handed down the tales of these ancestors from generation to generation. At one point Levi separates the first group of characters from the second by using the words "mythical characters" to refer to the first group. The second group is distinguished by the fact that they are only one or two generations removed from his own, so even if he had never met them (with the exception of his paternal grandmother), a stronger claim for truth is made for them.

If Levi's "relatives" are not ancestors, they are perhaps, *alla lunga,* more literary "characters," in the Italian sense of *personaggi,* than anything else. The Italian word *personaggio* demonstrates the connection between the character, the mask that promotes the existence of the character, and the larger world that the character inhabits, whether the world of the text or the visual world of the stage. The origins of the word *persona* (*person* in English) outlined in the *Vocabolario Etimologico della Lingua Italiana di Ottorino Pianigiani* reveal this more expansive meaning and also allow us to better understand Levi's use of *personaggi* in "Argon":

> The Latins called *person* (from per-sonar, to resound through) the wooden mask always worn by actors in the theaters of ancient Greece and in Italy. In these the facial features were exaggerated so that they could be better seen by the spectators and the mouth was made in such a way as to reinforce the sound of the voice (*ut personaret*): this was necessary because of the usual vastness of ancient theaters. This word then became used to mean the individual represented in the scene that now we call *personaggio*: then (the definition that persists today) any man, and subsequently his physique or the whole of his qualities.[56]

The wooden mask creates the character, and also allows for its public exposition. The word for "mask," interestingly, is a description of its function – "resounds through" – rather than a physical description. Performing through a series of displacements and metonymical associations, the word for mask is the function of the mask, which in turn becomes the character that the mask represents. The mask is specifically designed to promote and disseminate the character through its mouth being specially cut so to make the voice louder and more easily heard in a large public space. The word always hearkens back to theatricality, to the function of resounding. A persona (person), therefore, can only be a public self, antithetical to the notion of a private self.

The character in its masking, exaggeration, and staging thus becomes larger than life, just as anecdotes over time can take on larger dimensions and a theatrical quality. Levi's characters in "Argon" demonstrate these features, as they are represented through outrageous and obviously embellished anecdotes about their behaviour, and in some cases vivid descriptions of what they looked like or the Piedmontese/Hebrew jargon that they spoke. Considering Levi's relatives/characters as *personaggi* speaks to the nature of his fictive constructions in this chapter, and the staging that he creates for them.

The epic style narrative masks the private self that lies behind it, as well as highlighting his self-presentation as a narrator rather than an autobiographer. The lines are blurred between *person* conceived as a historical individual and *personaggio* as a fictive creation. *Person* as mask thus becomes the trope for fiction: both for the characters Levi creates and for the narrator himself. It also becomes the dominant trope for this recounting of Piedmontese Jewish history.

What lies behind these masks, however, is in the end more unsettling than entertaining: as it turns out, Levi's rendition of "family" history is fictive in omission as well as in detail. Levi invents stories about far-fetched "relatives" that constitute the community of Jews in Piedmont over a period of several hundred years, but he does not disclose a closer family history that would strike much closer to home for a victim of the persecution of the Holocaust. His actual family history contradicts his entertaining stories of the community described in "Argon"; as he says about them, "no stories of notable persecutions have been handed down."

The only example Levi gives of antisemitism during his father's childhood in the small town of Bene Vagienna is a ritualistic greeting mocking Jews wearing the prayer shawl that his schoolmates used to give his father. Levi describes this gesture as a remnant of intolerance, mocking but "benignly." It is a puzzling description, as mocking usually contains elements of malice or at the very least hostility. His description suggests that the mocking is devoid of real content, a remnant of the past that no longer has meaning.

At this point in his story, Levi is speaking about his own family as he mentions stories from his father, Giuseppe, and his paternal grandparents. The closer the reader gets to Levi's immediate family, the more intense the narrative masking becomes. The following is Levi's version of how his grandmother became a widow:

> In her good days she was known as *la Strassacoeur*, the Heartbreaker: she became a widow very early, and the rumor was that my grandfather had killed himself in despair because of her infidelities. In Spartan fashion she raised three children and educated them, but at an advanced age she let herself marry an old Christian doctor, majestic, bearded, and taciturn, and from then on she inclined to avarice and strangeness.[57]

The episode not mentioned in this chapter (nor anywhere else in Levi's work) is the fuller story of his grandmother's widowhood. Levi's paternal grandfather Michele and his great-grandfather Giuseppe had owned a family bank in Bene Vagienna in the latter part of the nineteenth century. In July 1888, as the bank was recovering from some economic hardship along with the rest of the region, the family was forced out of business. Ian Thomson discusses the episode at some length in his biography of Levi, and recounts that a rumour of unknown origin was spread that the bank was failing, a self-fulfilling prophecy that resulted in a catastrophic run on the bank. Using anti-semitic rhetoric, a Domenican friar named Pietro Dompè incited mobs and ran the Jewish family out of town. Dompè's motives became clear when he subsequently opened his own bank in the same town. Levi's great-grandfather Giuseppe came close to being lynched by an angry mob, and his son, Levi's grandfather Michele, committed suicide at age thirty-nine after the family took refuge with relatives in Turin.[58] A lynch mob went after Giuseppe a second time only four days after Michele's suicide. A newspaper report shortly thereafter made it clear that the bank had not been in trouble before these assaults and that it was the efforts of the priest – in particular, his stirring up a mob – that caused the closure of the bank.

The precise relationship of Michele Levi's suicide to his wife's rumoured infidelities and the loss of the family business (and subse-quent need to leave the town) is not completely clear, but it appears that the antisemitism the family suffered and the subsequent closing of the bank was the immediate catalyst for this tragedy, as reported in a local paper. These disquieting and alarming facts regarding the Levi's "integration" into the town of Bene Vagienna stand in sharp contrast to the benign and idiosyncratic picture of Jewish life in the Piedmont countryside that Levi draws for us.

What is most striking about the rendition of Levi's family story in "Argon" is thus what is missing rather than what is articulated. The Bene Vagienna episode clearly constitutes a case of "notable perse-cution," to use Levi's own term, yet it is omitted in favour of a more benign framing of the tale. In Levi's story of his grandmother, more questions are raised than answered in his version of events. What were her motivations in marrying a non-Jew after the persecution and sui-cide of her Jewish husband, and why does Levi describe this as "letting herself marry" ("si lasciò sposare")? Why does she become a pathologi-cal miser after marrying the second husband? Levi's version is some-what different from the story we read in his biography. According to Thomson's sources, Adela was having a long-term affair with the doc-tor, and married him very shortly after the death of her husband, caus-ing some scandal in the town. Perhaps instead "letting oneself" is what Levi does not want to do: in other words, ceding to a more historically accurate picture of his family's failed integration by looking at the case of a very notable persecution.

Levi's recasting of this story demonstrates his desire to see these episodes not as representative of what was actually a difficult and troublesome integration into Piedmont, and therefore also reflective of the situation of Jews in Italy at this time, but rather as a witty, idiosyncratic recounting of his family's troubles.[59] His cultural analysis of the relationship of the Jewish community to the larger society is predicated on a belief that, like the mocking of his father's schoolmates, there is no actual malice found in exercising old forms of prejudice. The fascist era proved him quite wrong on this count.

The Periodic Table is arguably an autobiography of his own life as a chemist, despite his statements to the contrary, yet he begins with these Jewish ancestors and the resistance against their integration into their life in Piedmont. This sets the tone for the chapters to follow, some of which engage his own tense negotiation with fascist Italy, postwar adjustments, and a chapter in which he recounts an episode in Auschwitz. *The Periodic Table* is one of Levi's most revealing texts, for what it says about Jewish identity in "Argon," and for the ways in which he sets up strategies of narration that are brilliantly innovative and demonstrate his writerly persona to great advantage.

Conclusion

The Jewish part of Levi's cultural identity poses particular challenges: how does being persecuted as a Jew confer Jewish identity, and what are the ramifications of such an identity formation? What does actual religious belief have to do with the fact of persecution? In an interview, Ferdinando Camon asks if Levi is a believer. Levi responds that he is not and never has been, would like to be, but cannot manage it. Camon then quite reasonably asks him about his Jewishness, presuming a connection between lack of faith in God and his religion. Levi responds with one of his most evocative remarks regarding his Jewish identity:

> A purely cultural fact. If not for the racial laws and the concentration camp, I probably would no longer be a Jew, except for my last name. Instead this dual experience, the racial laws and the concentration camp, stamped me the way you stamp a steel plate: At this point I am a Jew, they've sewn the star of David on me and not only on my clothes.[60]

The internalized identity of persecution penetrates much deeper than an external symbol. The use of the yellow star during the Holocaust was a perversion and degradation of the Star of David, a symbol standing for the Jewish people: when sewn onto clothing, it becomes a mark not of religious belief but of racialist persecution and of victimization.

If this degraded form of the star is sewn into his very being, as Levi suggests, a deep conundrum is sewn along with it: that of the binding of persecution with a cultural and religious symbol, therefore suggesting the impossibility of a Jewish identity not bound up with persecution and with memory. Like the carving of memory into the heart Levi advocates in his version of the *Sh'ma*, persecution carves its place as well. This situation goes beyond the injunction of Jewish cultural memory, and constitutes a reformulation of what Jewish identity can mean after the Shoah.

Our understanding of Levi's Jewish identity needs to be tempered by the strategies he employs to contain the antisemitism he experienced in fascist Italy before the Holocaust. What were the stakes for Levi in viewing antisemitism under fascism as "superficial and inconsistent"? One can only speculate that the *italianità* of his identity was deeply unsettled by rising antisemitism in Italy. Feeling himself to be foremost an Italian, he could not reconcile this self-image with the realities of exclusion and betrayal that was fascist Italy for Italian Jews after the mid-1930s. The late-nineteenth-century genealogy of bigotry apparent in Levi's own family can be seen as a precursor to what was to come two generations later. Rather than the "lowest ebb" of antisemitism that Levi describes in his talk given to the Jewish community in 1939, he finds himself in the middle of a culmination that was not by any means a historical anomaly ascribable to Hitler's influence on Mussolini, a myth now largely debunked by scholars.[61]

Levi's Jewish identity, one not definable by the quantity of Jewish content in his works, nor only through self-affirmation or self-representation, is a complex structure that requires a diligent and broad approach to understanding its dimensions and its ramifications. In the end, the complicated ways in which Levi articulates this identity are emblematic of a self in part formulated by persecution and in part by the post-Holocaust condition. Levi's Jewish identity is inextricably tied to his fate as a writer and as a witness, subject positions that I turn to in the following chapters.

Chapter Three

Primo Levi's Writerly Identity: From Science to Storytelling

Levi's career as writer was multifaceted and very rich, as he tried his hand at various genres and modes. As well as his Holocaust memoirs, he wrote fiction ranging from science fiction fantasies to a novel about Jewish partisans, essays, and poetry that varies from very dark to experimental and humorous, as well as publishing the picaresque tale of his return to civilization, *The Reawakening*, in 1958. Eventually he wrote the story of his life as a chemist, *The Periodic Table* (1975), which received great critical acclaim and was the reason for Levi's enormous popularity in the United States after the translation was published in 1984.[1] He ended his career with his groundbreaking and widely cited book of essays of 1984, *The Drowned and the Saved*. Another major work, entitled *The Double Bond*, was planned but not completed at the time of his death in 1987.

An aspect of Levi's career that is worth considering is how Levi as a writer engaged with the Italian literary canon, or rather failed to do so. Giuseppe Tosi comments that critics did not know what to do with Levi for a long time, as he did not fit into any clear generic, aesthetic, or ideological categories, and states that "there was uneasiness on the part of the Italian left to revisit the Italian Shoah, mainly dictated by the political will to adhere to a specific antifascist historiography of WW II." The Italian left did not want to confront the reality of the Shoah in Italy, and Levi's concept of the grey zone directly challenged myths about resistance.[2] The historian Anna Bravo analyses the difficult subject position of Italian deportees when they returned from the camps: were they political activists, to be considered alongside partisans? Once it became clear that they had been deported for being Jews, not necessarily for being activists, their stories were shunted into the background in favour of a political discourse that would emphasize heroism.[3]

From the very beginning of his writing career, Levi actively integrated his identity as a chemist with his emerging identity as a writer. Hayden White persuasively argues that Levi deliberately fosters a representation of himself as a writer based on scientific objectivity, widely accepted by critics:

> He believed that the kinds of scientific procedures he learned as a student of chemistry (weighing, measuring, breaking compounds down into basic elements and then reassembling them into different combinations) could serve him adequately for observing the events of the camps as they really were and not as either desire or prejudice would wish them to be. And in his writing, Levi tried to develop a mode of exposition equivalent to the kind of quantitative idiom chemists used to record changes and stabilities in chemical compounds. I find it remarkable and, in the present context, of distinct theoretical interest that Levi's characterization of the style of writing he wished to cultivate for giving a responsible and rational account of the camp experience – all focused on the ideals of clarity, measure, and exactitude – has been so uncritically accepted by commentators on his work.[4]

Indeed, Levi's identity as a writer cannot be separated from his self-conception as a chemist, although that particular relationship is over-determined because of his own self- representation. I will consider the formation of his writerly identity as bound up with that of the scientist, looking at the ways in which Levi's scientific self affected and determined the view of his writing that he chose to put forward. White's assertion that Levi believed scientific procedures were adequate for impartial observation needs to be looked at very carefully: is this Levi's actual belief, or is it the self-representation of himself as a writer that he wished to present to the world?

There are several crucial stages in his development as a writer that I will discuss: first the emergence of the testimonial impulse, then his developing view of style and perspective in *Survival in Auschwitz*, and finally an analysis of one of his science fiction stories in order to see how the fictive mode suited his portrayal of science in the Holocaust. Critical approaches to Levi also need to be part of this discussion, as they have widely influenced the reception of his texts, and betray some assumptions about Holocaust literature in general and Levi in particular that are important to examine.

Testimonial Beginnings and the Scientific Mode

Ian Thomson, in his biography of Levi, recounts how Levi began telling his testimony to whoever would listen:

> Soon he was talking to strangers on the trams and buses that were beginning to run again, reporting his story to anyone who cared to listen. The compulsion to do so was "as strong as hunger," Levi recalled ... Primo saw himself a storyteller returned from the edge of civilization with urgent counsel for his listeners.[5]

Levi's choice of how to write about his experiences was directly linked to his need to talk about them. According to Thomson, at some later point in his life Levi created a legend about the urgency of the telling of his story, asserting that he began writing on the way back to Italy. But facts dictate otherwise: the book was actually begun several months after his return home, and was a laborious process rather than a story that sprang into being. Levi seems to have rehearsed its composition by talking through his experiences, not only to strangers but also to his friends.[6]

Levi states clearly, on more than one occasion, that he found writing to be liberating, a crucial step in his recovery after his time in Auschwitz. Ferdinando Camon, in one of the most important interviews ever conducted with him, asks him how this inner liberation worked: was Levi's writing for the purpose of denouncing the Nazis, achieving justice? To understand the mystery of how the genocide could have taken place? Consolation? Levi's response is most intriguing:

> I wrote because I felt the need to write ... I've had the feeling that for me the act of writing was equivalent to lying down on Freud's couch. I felt such an overpowering need to talk about it that I talked out loud. Back then, in the concentration camp, I often had a dream: I dreamed that I'd returned, came home to my family, told them about it, and nobody listened. The person standing in front of me doesn't stay to hear, he turns around and goes away. I told the dream to my friends in the concentration camp, and they said, "It happens to us too." ... Later I chose to write it as the equivalent of talking about it.[7]

Levi presents us with an apparently seamless transition from the concept of *talking* about his experiences in Auschwitz, expressed as a need so strong as to be primal, to the act of *writing* about them. His remarks also reveal another transition, from the individual who speaks of his own experience to the expressive needs of the other survivors. On his return from Auschwitz, Levi became a writer in order to put forward what he had been through, his own suffering. But he also wanted to articulate what the entire community had endured. In an interview in 1984, he comments, "if there is an impulse behind my writing, it is linked to my deportation, to the suffering of others."[8] He began thinking about the writing of *Survival in Auschwitz* on his way home, that ten-month journey after the arrival of the Russians at Auschwitz that led him on a meandering journey through parts of eastern Europe before making it back to Turin. He had taken notes while still in the camp that had to be destroyed immediately, for their discovery would have put his life in great danger.

In his afterword to the interview, Camon discusses Levi's profound influence as a writer of both literature and testimony. I would assert that Levi's focus was not so much to set literature apart from testimony but quietly to insist on high literary standards within his testimony. This enterprise, however, is not without complexity. Levi's emphasis on a seamless evolution between talking and writing, and between the first-person and the plural representation, reflects an important concern he confronts as a writer: how to make testimony seem transparent so that literary strategies do not appear to detract from the main message. His representation of the origin of the testimony as a spontaneous creation rather than a rehearsed and carefully constructed text reflects that same desire. At the same time, he believed in the engagement of the deepest possible thought about the subject, using literary metaphors to universalize and to embrace a very broad humanistic set of concerns, yet all the while trying to follow the dictates of a transparent testimony. The tensions between these modes bring to the forefront a number of other issues, including the complicated relationship between autobiography and testimony, to be explored in the next chapter.

Before we look at Levi's writing strategies in his main testimonial work, *Survival in Auschwitz*, it's crucial to examine his very first publication in order to understand his itinerary as a developing writer. In 1946 he co-authored an essay with fellow survivor Leonardo Benedetti entitled "Rapporto sulla organizzazione igienico-sanitario del campo di concentramento per Ebrei di Monowitz (Auschwitz-Alta Silesia)" (Report on the Hygenic and Sanitary Organization of the Monowitz Concentration Camp for Jews at Auschwitz-Upper Silesia). The report, published in a medical journal entitled *Minerva medica*, originated with a request from the Soviet government to describe the sanitary conditions at Auschwitz, including those found in the infirmary. Focusing on the community of victims, the essay seeks to describe the lack of sanitation, hygiene, and medical assistance at Auschwitz, and it also outlines the gas chambers, which Levi does not discuss elsewhere in his writings.

This publication demonstrates some of the concerns he will develop in *Survival in Auschwitz*, and speaks as well to his developing identity as a scientist writer and as a witness. The report in *Minerva medica* functions as a bridge between Levi's prewar identity as a chemist, his new identity as a survivor, and the writerly self that he develops after the war. His subject position as a commentator on science is established in this text, even though the report goes beyond what we normally think of as the boundaries of scientific reporting, through the cultural and structural analysis performed by its two authors.

Why was Levi, a chemist, involved in commenting on what are essentially medical issues? The answer is straightforward, at least from one point of view: Levi tells us in *The Reawakening* that he volunteered to work as a pharmacist in the transit camp of Katowice, in which he stayed on his way back to Italy. He did this on the advice of his friend Leonardo De Benedetti, following a certain logic, learned at Auschwitz, that it was best to be perceived as useful. At Katowice he was accepted as a medical professional because of a linguistic confusion: the Soviet authorities conflated the term "doctor," in Levi's case meaning his degree in chemistry, with "medical doctor." Levi then ended up helping Leonardo, who was in fact a physician, in the infirmary, thus conferring upon himself a new pseudo-identity as a doctor for the duration of his stay at the transit camp.The main part of the report is a recounting of the most common diseases found in the camp and their treatment, including an assessment of the hospital in Monowitz, one of the approximately forty subcamps that made up the Auschwitz complex. Elaborated in great detail, this part of the text furnishes the information that was requested by the Soviet goverment. The report, however, goes beyond simple description of the diseases that occurred and how they were handled. The authors also present an analysis of the structures involved: the logic of the response to these diseases and to general sanitary conditions. To cite just one example, the authors describe the "treatment" of patients afflicted with certain diseases, even if long cured:

As to syphilis, tuberculosis and malaria, we are not able to give any data as to their frequency since the syphilitic, the tubercular and the malarial – the latter even if long since cured and accidentally found out through their own incautious confession – were immediately dispatched to Birkenau and eliminated there in the gas chambers. It cannot be denied that this was a radical prophylactic method![9]

As a contribution to what was known about the camps in 1946, the report is extremely important, not only for its information about the organization of the camp but also because of the way in which the two authors frame the content. Robert Gordon, in the introduction to the 2006 English translation of the report, remarks that this framing is "strikingly, exceptionally clear ... describing its subject-matter immediately as 'the annihilation of the European Jews,' when this kind of description was far from common, decades before Holocaust studies were established as a discipline."[10]

There are other aspects of the report that are worth considering in the context of Levi's developing identity as a writer. The journal itself is a startling place to find such an article: as a premier medical journal in Italy, it could perhaps best be compared to the *New England Journal of Medicine* in the United States. Finding an essay on Auschwitz between its pages must have come as a surprise – perhaps a rather unpleasant one – to the physicians who made up the bulk of its readership.

I encountered the original of this report many years ago, an experience that reveals some aspects to it that are not immediately evident when it is read in its current republished form. Because *Minerva medica* is a well-known medical journal, piles of old, unbound, yellowed, and rather bedraggled issues stretching all the way back to 1946 and even before were sitting on shelves in the stacks at the Harvard Medical Library in Boston. Finding what was esssentially a first edition of Levi's first published work in such a place was extraordinary, especially given the other contents of the 24 November issue in which the report appeared.

Minerva medica's title page announced the name of the journal and stated that it was a publication intended for the practising physician. Levi and DeBenedetti's report was found somewhere in the middle, next to an article on viral pneumonia and secondary postpartum hemmorhaging. There was no editor's introduction to the report, or for that matter any other acknowledgment that the report was perhaps something unique or different from the other specialized articles in this very technical journal. The title of the report certainly stood out from the others, both in its mentioning of Auschwitz and in its absence of mention of a medical condition or disease, but the context in which it was found, the journal, was unself-consciously medical and scientific.

The overall effect was ultimately quite unsettling: the report, read as part of this journal, appears less scientific than the other articles, and thus seemed marginalized. Other issues from the same time period did not include articles of historical or cultural content offering a broad interpretation. Instead, the other publications resembled the ones contained in the issue in which Levi and DeBenedetti published their report: for the most part, descriptions of new treatments for disease.

There is a feeling of tension and anxiety produced by the appearance of their report in such a context. It is as if this was the only venue in which someone might listen to what Levi and DeBenedetti had to say: other doctors, who would be interested to know how disease was handled at Auschwitz. But why would these doctors be interested? The cover of *Minerva medica*, as noted above, describes itself as a "weekly gazette for the practicing physician." One wonders what effect the information contained in the Levi/DeBenedetti report would have had on the medical practices of the doctors reading it, as one would hope the information would not be practically useful to them.

Instead, the presence of this report in the journal functions as a *faits divers*, a kind of curious back-page news item. Furthermore, we might be tempted to speculate on the connections between Levi and DeBenedetti's decision to publish this report in such a journal, the refusal of major publishers to publish *Survival in Auschwitz* a few months later, and the recurring dream that Levi had while in the camp of returning home and finding no one willing to listen to his story. Can the venue of this publication be read as an indication of their feeling that no one else would be interested in this story? As Gordon comments, "like other survivors, De Benedetti and Levi were speaking, but not necessarily being heard."[11]

The critic Alberto Cavaglion was the first to discover this long-forgotten publication, and in 1991 he published an introduction that also contained the entirety of the report. He asks compelling questions regarding the establishment of Levi's writerly identity in relation to his scientific identity, stating: "the memoir [*memoriale*] demonstrates that the urge to tell the story was placated by the only venue that Levi considered authoritative, namely a scientific journal. The profession of science, from the start, won out over any 'other trade.'"[12] Cavaglion focuses on which writerly image Levi was trying to convey, rather than the inappropriateness of this journal as the place to publish such a report.

Interestingly, Cavaglion uses a word to describe the text that in some respects stands in opposition to the report's scientific and factual basis, calling it a *memoriale*, a word that in Italian has two meanings. The first and principal definition is "memoir" but, compellingly, the word has a secondary meaning, that of "petition to the court." The legalistic meaning of this word adds a juridical aspect: the evidentiary aspects of the report are crucial, and clearly one of the reasons that Levi and De Benedetti wanted to publish this article.

Both Cavaglion and Gordon point out similarities between the first and last chapters of *Survival in Auschwitz* and this report in *Minerva medica*. The report can be viewed as a rehearsal for his fully articulated testimony that did not have the strictures of a scientific journal as its place of publication. It reveals that Levi's urge to tell the story can be articulated in different ways, including a demonstration of his ability to remain distant from the text while using powerful metaphors to animate it.

The medical report shows not only the degree to which his identity as a scientist would dictate the beginning of a writing career, but also the ways in which Levi negotiates multiple identity positions in order to embark on this vocation. Levi the mature writer has not thus far fully emerged from the trauma of his experience. In the *Minerva medica* report, we find a factual recounting of the conditions of death and disease, and an analysis of the underlying "logic" of the Nazis in the set-up of the infirmary, but not yet an analysis of the effect of the camps on the human spirit. The bigger picture – the whys and wherefores of the organization of the camp and its intended result of not only murder but dehumanization, with ensuing implications for our understanding of humanity – will have to wait until Levi finishes the writing of *Survival in Auschwitz* and publishes it one year later.[13]

Survival in Auschwitz: Between Testimony and Literature

Survival in Auschwitz, published with some difficulty in 1946, is Levi's best-known work and one of the two best-known Holocaust testimonies in existence, second only to Elie Wiesel's *Night* in terms of sheer numbers of books published and languages into which the work has been translated. It is important, in looking at *Survival in Auschwitz* as Levi's first major publication, to ask who its intended audience was, and who were the intended protagonists of the story. For whom was Levi writing, and from what subject point of view was he writing: which subjects does his writing self encompass? The initial point of encounter between two forms of testimony – an oral form, which Levi practised at the outset of his writing career by talking to whomever would listen, and a literary approach – is found in the very question of whom the writing represents. For that reason, it is important to begin with the issue of perspective – who is represented by Levi's testimony, how is their voice heard – and then proceed to the question of what is at stake in this choice.

A conscientious and deliberate use of the personal pronoun "I," versus the collective "we," marks tension between the text's obligation as testimony and its obligation as autobiography, conceived as a more personal witnessing. The choice of the pronoun referring to the writer, plural or singular, can either create or eliminate distance between the writer and the reader. As Robert Gordon comments, "Indeed, in some ways, the defining characteristic of [Levi's] style is its somewhat laboured, rather formal aspect which creates an interesting, fertile distance between the narrative voice and its medium."[14]

This distance is indeed fertile, because it points to some deeper issues regarding his authorial voice. Levi's need to perform collective witnessing becomes apparent very early in his text. In order to find such a passage, we need look no further than the end of the preface to *Survival in Auschwitz*. Even though Levi begins with his own personal story, he makes clear his focus on the collective nature of the experience:

> I recognize, and ask indulgence for, the structural defects of the book. Its origins go back, if not in practice, as an idea, an intention, to the days in the Lager. The need to tell our story to "others," to make "others" share it, took on for us, before the liberation and after, the character of an immediate and violent impulse, to the point of competing with other elementary needs. The book was written to satisfy that need: in the first place, therefore, as an interior liberation. Hence its fragmentary character: the chapters were written not in logical succession but in order of urgency. The work of linking and unifying was carried out more deliberately, and is more recent."[15]

Levi begins this discussion using the first person pronoun in his statement "I ... ask indulgence for," but then embraces the inclusiveness of the plural with the use of "us" as he discusses the need that survivors have to tell the story, to make others witness the destruction. He initially takes responsibility for the book's flaws, yet his following disclaimer about these flaws pulls in the entire survivor community, as if to say: We are all alike in this inadequacy. Testimony is from us, not from me, and is to satisfy a burning need that we all have. Emphasized by his use of passive constructions ("the book was written," "the chapters were written"), this collective concept is also employed in his recounting of the shared dream of needing to tell the story, yet not being heard in that telling, mentioned in the interview with Camon and recounted at length in *Survival in Auschwitz*.

The seed of Levi's narrative is thus not the urge of the individual to tell his or her story, which we can identify as an autobiographical impulse, but rather the common need of the community. Furthermore, the story is told for *others*, a term he puts between quotation marks in both occurrences, as if to distinguish between the "others" who were persecuted and a new category of "other," those who were not persecuted but need to be pulled into the story, need to participate in it, even at the expense of eliding the first person and neglecting the script of autobiography. At this point, our subjects are three in number: Levi the individual, the other victims and survivors whom he wants to represent, and his reading audience.

It is significant that Levi uses the word *partecipe* to refer to readers, to others. *Partecipe* in Italian is similar to "participate" in English, but can also mean to share, to communicate, even just to be physically present, such as "ho partecipato allo sposalizio," I was present at the wedding. If we look at Levi's use of *partecipe* as sharing, this can go both directions: others, non-survivors, can share in the experience of writing, a writing performed by the author who is simultaneously sharing the need to write with other survivors as he shares the content of that experience with another plural group, his reading public: this public is thus raised to become readers/participants who are actively present at the side of the text, witnessing through their reading.

Once he begins *Survival in Auschwitz*, Levi strongly prefers the "we" to the "I." The following passage speaks directly to the issue of connecting the reader with the text in a forceful manner that makes clear his goal of representing the group. This passage is found in the second chapter of *Survival in Auschwitz*, entitled "On the Bottom":

Imagine now a man who has been deprived of everyone he loves, and at the same time of his house, his habits, his clothes, of literally everything, in short, that he possesses: he will be a hollow man, reduced to suffering and needs, heedless of dignity and restraint, for he who loses everything can easily lose himself. He will be a man whose life or death can be lightly decided, with no sense of human affinity – in the most fortunate case, judged purely on the basis of utility. It is in this way that one can understand the double meaning of the term "extermination camp," and it will be clear what we seek to express with the phrase "lying on the bottom."[16]

In sum, Levi's identity as a writer, in his first major text, is defined in large part by whom he wants to represent. This point cannot be made strongly enough, as it speaks to both his motivation as a writer and his style. His identity is fashioned as well by his ability to make his readers present in the text, as he asks us to imagine what it was like to actually be there: to *participate* to the extent to which this is possible for a reader.

Levi and the Question of Style

The multitude of reasons for the immense popularity of *Survival in Auschwitz* as testimony and as literature have been widely discussed in Levi criticism. These discussions, however, have focused more on the effects of his text than on the precise ways in which the text produces those effects. In fact, readers and many critics have often been so unaware of Levi's literary strategies that it is instructive to explore this failure to notice his style. Both the reception of his texts and Levi's own statements on writing, compared against how his texts actually work as literature, not only illustrate a deep paradox of representation but also bring to light other issues, including what readers actually want to find in a text about the Holocaust and how those desires influence the reception of the text.[17]

Quite often, critical reception of Levi approvingly points to his objectivity, his "dispassionate" witnessing, and his ability to universalize, to delineate and to explore a broad humanistic context within which to examine the moral and ethical questions that arise from a study of the Shoah. Levi's scientific training is often singled out as permitting him to take a long view, to write in a style that Irving Howe called "unadorned and chaste"[18] and that Cynthia Ozick described as "lucid and calm," demonstrating "magisterial equanimity."[19] These assessments reflect more the desire of the reader to find certain qualities in Levi's texts than the reality of what is actually in the texts. There is a lot at stake here, as the reader wishes the survivor/writer to be objective and to convey the reality of the camps with lucidity. This is not to say that these descriptions are inaccurate, but rather that they are unnecessarily limiting and suggest transparency: "unadorned" implies a paucity of style and "chaste" a lack of emotion.

Among critics who look more closely at the production of meaning in Levi's texts, there are two in particular who illustrate the complex meanings of Levi's text and argue against reading him as transparent. In an excellent essay regarding what he calls Levi's "ethical uncertainty," Bryan Cheyette, like Hayden White, persuasively argues against a simplistic view of Levi as a dispassionate, detached narrator. Cheyette looks at what he calls the "painful ambiguity of Levi's task," as Levi needed to balance the exigencies of commemorative remembrance against the demands of storytelling, concluding that Levi had an "inability to settle on any one way of telling his story."[20] Another equally persuasive view, however, would be an understanding of Levi as a writer with a multiplicity of voices for whom that multiplicity was a way of exploring his skill. It is important to point out that neither approach to the question of Levi's multiple narrating personas provides a definitive answer: what can be seen as an inability to make a single choice can also be seen as a rich experimentation. The fact that Levi's narrative choices can be read both ways is significant in itself, and points to the complex nature of his texts.

Another critical approach is to assume that Levi had complete control over his texts. Elizabeth Scheiber asserts that Levi is able in *The Periodic Table* to "unite his different selves, using chemistry as a link between his identity before, during and after his experiences at Auschwitz."[21] Her analysis has much merit, as Levi certainly uses chemistry as a common link. Yet Scheiber betrays a telling expectation of unity in Levi's works, as if Levi, who has indeed created so many moments of absolute clarity and comprehension in his works, would always and invariably produce unity, that contradictions and complications cannot exist in Levi's works except insofar as they constitute controlled moments of his arguments. This is a commonly found attitude towards Levi's work.[22] Often assumptions are made about Levi that range from taking him at face value to a presumed authorial omniscience. This is not to say that all Levi criticism falls into these categories, but there is a remarkable pattern, as I have briefly outlined.[23] Domenico Scarpa has remarked, "Perhaps the mistake of the critics has been not so much a lack of understanding of how Levi's texts function, but of how Levi functions."[24]

Despite these apparent limitations, the body of Levi criticism is overall quite astute and perceptive about the enormous value of Levi's writings.[25] It seems, however, that the more the writer is esteemed for his brilliant analyses, the more reluctance there is to examining the rhetorical structures that make this depth possible.

It is without question that many commentators have taken Levi at his word about how he writes. But even in White's important analysis of Levi's figural style, in which he argues so cogently against taking Levi at face value, there are two apparent blind spots. The first is about the definition of figural language: is it all to be lumped together? The second moment lies in what Levi *says* versus how he actually *practises* writing: in other words, his beliefs regarding his statements about writing in relation to his self-representation as a writer.

Stating that Levi openly eschewed all figural modes of writing, White says:

> Much of this commentary presumes that these ideals can be achieved only by cleaving to an impossibly rigorous ideal of literalist expression, a speech voided of figurative usage and a language utterly purged of "rhetorical" tropes.[26]

There is distance, however, between Levi's insistence on language that communicates and the claim that he rejected all figural language. It appears that the presumption underlying this statement is that all figural language is the same, and so Levi rejected all of it. Yet this rejection is inconsistent with an author who freely cites Dante and other highly figural texts.

After ably demonstrating in his essay that Levi's writing is indeed highly figural, White states that Levi sees writing and figural language as incompatible:

> Levi's own writing practices run directly counter to his stated aim as a stylist. His writing is consistently and brilliantly figurative throughout and, far from being void of rhetorical flourishes and adornments, constitutes a model of how a specifically literary mode of writing can heighten both the referential and the semantic valences of a discourse of fact.[27]

Levi's "own stated aim as a stylist" is precisely the issue here. Levi's writing is anything but straightforward exposition, as White demonstrates by looking at the complex figural language that Levi employs in *Survival in Auschwitz*, in particular his use of Dante. White states that Levi gives himself authorial credibility through his connecting scientific method with the ability to give accurate and meaningful testimony. But oddly, as a conclusion White makes the following remark: "Levi believed that his was a style more scientific than artistic." After making a strong case for the sheer artistry of Levi's writings, White implies that Levi did not understand his own craft and was not a good reader of himself. He takes Levi at his word when he says, "Levi's own writing practices run directly counter to his stated aim as a stylist," as if this statement must lead to the conclusion that Levi actually *believed* his style was not particularly artistic. The second problem in this analysis, as I've remarked, lies in the distance between Levi's critique of writing that does not communicate well and the concept of figural language. Levi does not actually make statements against all figural language, only that language he views as too obscure. He desperately wants to communicate clearly with his reader, even through using language that is highly figural. To Levi there is a vast difference between citing Dante at apt moments and writing in the style of an author like Paul Celan, whom Levi believed to be obscure and unclear.[28]

Regarding Levi's own use of figural language, there are two possibilities here. The first is that Levi is so immersed in the culture of Dante that he does not see him as an author who fails to get his message across. The second possibility is that Levi creates a writing persona that, simply put, states one thing but does another, perhaps quite deliberately. This is the moment where the question of *multiple* writing personas comes into play, and the question of how Levi wanted to be perceived, as opposed to what he actually believed about writing.

There is no question that Levi represents himself as a chemist and survivor first and as a writer second. Yet if the contradictions found in what Levi says he is doing – namely a writing that is straightforward, chemical – and the actual writing are examined, another and generally unrecognized scenario becomes equally obvious. The usual path we think of for Levi, a story told by Levi himself, is that he was trained as a chemist in fascist Italy, was deported as an Italian Jew, became a Holocaust survivor, then became a writer because of a moral imperative to write following his experiences in the Holocaust. If, however, we look at Levi as a writer first and a chemist or survivor second or third, then both his texts and the way we need to read them acquire more clarity. It is in the particulars and subtleties of his texts that we see his writer's vocation as dominant, not an accident of circumstance as it is so often described by Levi himself and by others.

As White and other critics have pointed out, Levi himself advanced a certain view of his texts, even directly connecting his process of writing to scientific method and to chemical reaction in interviews and essays. Using chemistry as a metaphor, he commented on the similarities between the two trades, as words (elements) are carefully selected and distilled: "When someone asks me 'Why are you a chemist who writes?' I answer, 'I write because I am a chemist.' It is my profession that helps me to communicate my experience."[29] White points out that Levi rejects notions of modern literature that do not deliver their message in a straightforward manner, in, for example, his essay entitled "Communication" in *The Drowned and the Saved*. Levi has also gone on record many times as taking a stand against writing that is not clear and concise: "Both *If This Is a Man* and *The Truce* are written in a language that everyone can understand, in everyday speech. I believe it is the task of every writer to describe what he sees in plain language, and I hope I have achieved this."[30] He preferred writing to be straightforward and as transparent as possible, so that his testimony would also reflect this same transparency. In fact, he sometimes goes so far as to deny any active involvement of either style or literature, remarking in an interview that his testimony "was written without even a hint of literary worries: if there is literature there, it is unwanted, an intrusion. I certainly never considered problems of style."[31]

His own statements, however, sidestep a crucial issue in his writing and what can be understood as his style. It is precisely the encounter between writing that communicates clearly, as he puts it, and his own use of stylistic devices and figural language that he does not engage, either in his comments about the need for clarity or the ways in which chemistry and writing share common methods. There is only a hint of it in the way he discusses the language of chemistry, as he considers its symbolic value:

> Chemistry provided my subject matter for a book and two stories. I feel it in my hand as a reservoir of metaphors: the further away is the other field, the more taut the metaphor ... The fact is that anyone who knows how to reduce and concentrate, to distill and crystallize, also knows that laboratory operations have a long symbolic shadow.[32]

How immensely complicated and rich Levi's style turns out to be hides behind the screen of a purported transparency that utterly belies the depth of his writing. Indeed, how successful Levi was at projecting the image of clear, transparent writing on his part is clear by the aforementioned reception of his texts by many readers and critics. The ways in which the issue of style interrelates with his need to tell the story and create an audience needs to be foremost in a consideration of Levi's writing. He has been quite clear about for whom he writes: "It has to satisfy the reader. I don't write for myself, or if I do, I tear it up, I destroy what I've written. I think it's wrong to write for oneself. Of course, everyone is free to do as they please, it doesn't harm anyone, but it feels like time wasted to me."[33]

At the same time, Levi critics raise important questions through their assumptions about the nature of Levi's texts. Why did Levi find it necessary to hide his writing persona behind the screen of objectivity? The view of Levi as a writer who is driven not by questions of style and aesthetics but by "scientific objectivity" has made it difficult to appreciate the depth and breadth of his narrative voices. This view has, however, made it possible for the reader or the critic to accept complex figurative exposition on Levi's part as "scientific" or "detached."[34] Critics and readers are also driven by a strong desire to find order and unity in a text that represents the Holocaust and the Holocaust survivor: as will be explored below, the fragmented self that Levi ultimately displays in his writings is as chaotic and frightening as his subject matter.

Another factor in the reception of Levi's texts is what readers want and expect from Holocaust testimony. The attitude, often unwitting, that testimony is unmediated and transparent has deeply affected the ways in which Levi's writing is viewed, even those writings that are not testimonial. As critics have often noted, readers typically want the Holocaust text to provide a clearly articulated set of historical facts.[35] Considerations such as point of view and differences between individual experiences are glossed over in favour of empirical truth, as if the testimony were not a literary text, with all that implies regarding the use of language and the personal perspective of the writer.

Part of the issue lies with a set of assumptions regarding the nature of Holocaust literature and perceived "rules" regarding its composition. The noted historian Raul Hilberg comments, "The question is not confined to *what* we should describe, it is also a matter of *how* we should write. Are there any rules?"[36] The rules, spoken or unspoken, are driven by demands that any writing about the Holocaust must function as historical representation. As Berel Lang perceptively comments, "All Holocaust writing aspires to the condition of history," arguing as well that realism "has served the literary imagination as a figurative or stylistic 'choice' with no place for truth or falsity among its criteria ... The assessment of style, in other words, involves many but always other factors than the standard of truth or falsity."[37] Lang also raises the issue of the fictionalizations and omissions found in Levi's work, that constitute an important element of his theory and practice of writing.[38] Irving Howe believes that "Holocaust writings make their primary claim ... through facts recorded or remembered."[39]

Testimony in particular is the most vulnerable form of Holocaust writing when it comes to these "rules." The authority of testimony comes from an insistence that it be an "unvarnished" – or unstylized – truth. As Michael Andre Bernstein argues,

> One of the most pervasive myths of our era, a myth perhaps even partially arising out of our collective response to the horrors of the concentration camps, is the absolute authority given to first person testimony. Such narratives ... are habitually regarded as though they were completely unmediated, as though language, gesture and imagery could become transparent if the experience being expressed is sufficiently horrific.[40]

The Argentinian writer Nora Strejilevich, in her essay "Testimony: Beyond the Language of Truth," states:

> However, in spite of survivors' efforts to translate their memories, there is a distance between the way testimonies demand to voice their truth, and the expectations readers or listeners have regarding what truth means and how it should be voiced. Testimony, as every product in our culture, is often seen as a commodity that must provide practical use. Society wants to use witnesses' accounts as evidence, and testimonies are condemned in case they do not match evidence collected by other means.[41]

Given these considerations, it comes as little surprise that Levi would typically choose *not* to foreground the intense literariness of his text, and that his self-representation as a writer would emphasize the organic nature of his testimony rather than the complex literary structures that drive it. As Antony Rowland remarks in his excellent essay on Levi's poetry as a form of testimony:

> Levi employs the poetic technique of simile because prose testimony does more than simply recount specific facts. The genre is sometimes

assumed not to do so because of the term's origin in the juridical sense of a narrative which provides "attestation in support of a fact or statement" (OED, 2nd ed.).[42]

The Canto of Levi

Even more intensely constitutive of the formation of the writing subject in Primo Levi's case is the introduction of high literature, a strategy that Levi adopts that permeates *Survival in Auschwitz*. Citations from Dante and other great writers appear frequently in *Survival in Auschwitz*, and indeed form the organizing principle for one entire chapter, which I will discuss in some detail. But first some theoretical considerations are in order.

The notion that literary models can be an encumbrance or worse to Holocaust testimonies has been addressed by Lawrence Langer and other critics. Langer in particular makes a compelling argument about the interplay between survivor memoirs and traditional literary forms. In his discussion of to whom public memory of the Holocaust is best entrusted, he argues:

All of them re-create the details and images of the event through written texts, and in so doing remind us that we are dealing with *represented* rather than unmediated reality. For the critic and imaginative writer, this is obvious; for the historian and survivor, perhaps less so.[43]

Langer continues his argument by examining the ways in which survivor accounts, in their creation of the narrative, employ teleological views and what he calls "traditional literary associations." He also uses the term "deceptive continuities" to describe any association between the experiences of the camps and literary texts that may have served as models for survivor authors.

One of the examples he gives of such associations is Levi's well-known citation of Dante in the chapter entitled "The Canto of Ulysses" in *Survival in Auschwitz*. Levi makes many references to classical texts, and Dante is chief among his referents. Nowhere is Dante's figural hell more present than in "The Canto of Ulysses." Taking a close look at how Levi uses Dante brings out some of the issues regarding the relationship between testimony, literary standards, and the notion of writing as transparent or "straightforward." Levi's use of Dante can in fact be viewed as exemplary of some little-understood aspects of Levi's style. The problematic aspects that we find in his use allow us to understand that the perception of Levi's style as "straightforward" is a myth that significantly detracts from the richness and complexity of the text.

The chapter "Canto of Ulysses" is placed strategically, one of three that constitute the most intense part of Levi's testimony, forming a central portion of the text. The first of these three chapters is "The Drowned and the Saved," in which Levi presents four cases of moral ambiguity in relation to survival. He then continues to his own case of adaptive survival in the chapter that follows, entitled "Chemical Examination." In this episode, Levi's former identity as a chemist asserts itself long enough for him to pass an exam given by a German chemist who does not look at Levi as a fellow human being. Coming next, "The Canto of Ulysses" functions as a final episode and commentary on these chapters of intense moral exploration that also raise questions of Levi's own identity within the camp. As Sharon Portnoff comments in her analysis of the relationship of Levi's testimony to Dante, "Levi's use of Dante's poem serves not only to compare the experiences of prisoner and pilgrim, but also to suggest their utter incommensurability."[44] It is precisely this incommensurability that points out what is at stake in Levi's use of Ulysses as a figure of literary memory, that betrays as much as it evokes.

In "The Canto of Ulysses," Levi recounts walking with a camp friend to the soup kitchen, a long walk on a sunny day, constituting a brief respite from typical camp life. Levi has been released from heavy work detail for an hour to go and get soup for his group in the company of Jean the Pikolo, who has chosen him for this honour as his assistant. The weather is warmer than usual, and the two feel briefly liberated as they go on the long walk that will take them to the soup kitchen. Their trip to fetch the soup is initially contextualized within the story of whom they encounter on the walk. The trip is not without its hazards: along the way they meet an SS man and then a well-known spy, whom Levi tells us does evil for evil's sake.

After these preludes, the heart of the chapter is reached as Jean announces to Levi his desire to learn Italian: Jean has spent a month in Pisa and is attracted to the language. This seems to be a good way to spend this extra time they have found. But Levi is not content with a mere linguistic exercise in modern Italian: instead the great medieval poet Dante comes to mind, and then, for reasons Levi does not himself admit to understanding, the canto of Ulysses. From a pedagogical point of view, this is a rather odd choice for a language text, as

Dante's language, while indescribably beautiful, is also quite difficult and opaque. From the beginning it is clear that there is much more at stake than a language lesson. Elizabeth Scheiber discusses the significance of the role of Jean the Pikolo in this episode as a testament to the importance of listening, a task that Levi assigns to his reader as well.[45]

At first, Levi gives Jean (and us) Dante in the most generic terms: Virgil is Reason, Beatrice is Theology. But then he begins to cite:

Lo maggior corno della fiamma antica
Comincio' a crollarsi mormorando,
Pur come quella cui vento affatica.
Indi, la cima in qua e in la' menando
Come fosse la lingua che parlasse
Mise fuori la voce, e disse: Quando ...

The greater horn
Within that ancient flame
Began to sway and tremble
Murmuring,
Just like a fire that
Struggles in the wind;
then, he waved his
flame-tip back and forth
as if it were a tongue that
tried to speak,
And flung toward us a
voice that answered:
"When ..."[46]

This quotation is taken from canto 26, deep in the inferno, where Dante encounters Ulysses. Condemned to hell for being a false counsellor, Ulysses has used his intellect for his own self-interested ends. The Dantean *contrappasso* is the ancient flame, in which the soul of Ulysses is burning. The flame represents the tongue, language, that highest aspect of human intellect, because Ulysses has used his immensely skilful command of rhetoric to convince his men to follow him on one last and very perilous journey, to seek after knowledge. Levi then translates these lines into French for Jean, who helps him with the word "antica."

Levi's memory fails him, as he strives to remember what comes after that "when." After struggling with the lacuna for a while, he remembers a crucial line: "Ma misi me per l'alto mare aperto," but I set out on the open sea.[47] He tells us that he is sure of this line, that he is able to explain to Jean the Pikolo why it is that "misi me," I put myself forth, is so much stronger and more audacious than "je me mis, mi metto."

Suddenly the narrative is interrupted and they are out of Dante and back in the world of the camp, as they pass the Kraftwerk, the power plant. After a brief description of this place in which we leave the Dantean subtext completely, Levi goes back to struggling with his memory, and brings back only fragments of lines. An entire tercet, one of the most significant in the canto, subsequently comes to him and he asks Jean to pay attention, to open his ears and his mind. Framing it thus, he cites:

Considerate la vostra semenza:
Fatti non foste a viver come bruti,
Ma per seguir virtute e conoscenza.

Consider well the seed that gave you birth: you were not made to live your lives as brutes, but to be followers of worth and knowledge.[48]

As Lina Insana and Robert Gordon have pointed out, there is an echoing from Levi's poem "Shemà," the poem that serves as an epigraph to his testimony; Gordon has indeed drawn fascinating parallels between the two instances of "consider" in relation to Levi's memory project.[49] The poetic line is "considerate se questo è un uomo," consider if this is a man: also the title of his testimony. The connection between the two texts in fact goes much farther than this: Levi's poem "Shemà" demands the reader's attention by mirroring the prayer Sh'ma – listen, the call to monotheism. As Levi cites Dante's line in this chapter, an intense intertextual moment of reckoning is created, as the line refers simultaneously to Dante, to the Sh'ma prayer, and to Levi's own poem, which is a bold secular rewriting of the Sh'ma, in which the call to remember the Shoah is put forth as the major injunction to memory rather than a listening to God.

In the next moment in the testimony, Levi describes his own reaction to his citation of the Dantean lines in the following way, further strengthening the connection to the prayer Sh'ma: "As if I, too, were hearing it for the first time: like the blast of a trumpet, like the voice of God."[50] Clearly a Sh'ma-like revelatory moment that also evokes the sound of the blowing of the shofar, he then says, "For a moment I forget who I am and where I am."[51] The blowing of the shofar is a significant event for the Jewish world: used exclusively on Rosh Hashanah, the new year, and on Yom Kippur, the day of atonement, the shofar marks the new year as well as the opening and closing of the book of life.

Acknowledging the attention paid by Jean the Pikolo and the good it is doing Levi the narrator to be citing these passages, he also declares that perhaps it is because Pikolo has received the message: the book of life has been opened to him as well. According to Levi, Pikolo understands that this has to with him and with all who struggle, and he and Levi "who dare to talk about these things with the soup poles on our shoulders."[52]

The next Dantean line cited by Levi is "Li miei compagni fec'io sì acuti" (I made my comrades so eager), a boasting description of how ardent Ulysses's men were made by his speech about their need to search for knowledge and virtue, and clearly precisely the reaction Levi is receiving from Jean. Levi again struggles, in vain he says, with the word "acuti": how to translate that, how to convey the eagerness that the word signifies, thus emphasizing the power of language to seduce.

In the end, however, such rhetorical persuasion on the part of Ulysses proved fatal, as this voyage was their last and he and his men perished on the rocks, drawn in by another seduction, that of Circe. Levi cites as much as he can remember to his friend, with frequent lapses in his memory and an intense, close-to-desperate tone to his weaving of the two tales: one the fate of Ulysses, the other their trip to the soup kitchen.

The episode generates compelling questions concerning the use of high literature in testimony. How is the figure of Ulysses, often interpreted heroically, actually used in Levi's interpretation? How does Levi set up Dante's text as an imposed figural and literary language that he places within the context of a *real* hell? The figurative hell, set forth as the background for conversion and eventual salvation in Dante, sharply contrasts with the second, a literal hell that goes beyond the ability of language to describe it: a hell that cannot in any case, in any world, be redemptive.

The reception of this chapter has been almost as interesting and fraught with issues as the episode itself. Levi's use of high literature is often lauded as a sign of the secular humanism that allowed him a broad and expansive understanding of Western culture, a knowledge that informed his wisdom and sobriety when dealing with the serious matter of the Shoah. Most critics praise Levi's ability to recall the Dante and teach it to his friend; in fact, critical response to this chapter has been so laudatory as to verge on the hagiographic. The combination of Levi and Dante seems quite irresistible. Jonathan Druker, one of the few critics who sees an ambivalence in this episode, remarks that Ulysses is typically viewed as "an unproblematic standard bearer for Levi's humanism."[53] In fact, there appears to be quite a lot at stake here. Lina Insana asserts that a "dangerous realization" occurs because of the juxtaposition of Levi the prisoner with Levi the cultured self before his imprisonment, leading to a comprehension of the enormous distance between the two selves.[54]

In the view of many critics, Dante provides a recuperative, even redemptive moment for Levi; some go so far as to say that his very survival is linked to this dramatic re-enactment of an episode from another time and place. But at least one voice remains deeply sceptical of the combination of testimony and literary models. Lawrence Langer comments:

> I think the irony of this passage, whose content contrasts so visibly with the setting and with the scene, is explicit. For a moment both Levi and Jean, under the compelling sway of Dante's art, forget who and where they are. And this is precisely the point: when literary form, allusion, and style intrude on the surviving victim's account, we risk forgetting where we are and imagine deceptive continuities.[55]

It is essential to take a closer look at the notion of "deceptive continuities," for within lies the crux of the matter, and not only in terms of using literary models in testimony. An examination of continuities, deceptive or otherwise, may also shed light on Levi's view and theory of writing his testimony and his life story. Several questions suggest themselves: Are there indeed continuities established through references to great texts, and if so, what is their nature? Are they in fact deceptive, and if so, what does this deception mean? What are the consequences for the testimonial project?[56]

The first matter that should be raised in regard to the notion of deceptive continuities is: what happens if we deprive ourselves of great literary models? At the other end of the spectrum lies the well-rehearsed debate regarding the inherent defects of language in representing the Shoah. Most writers and critics openly acknowledge the difficulty of making words whose definitions we understand in the context of free society bend and perhaps break under the weight of an explanation of events that the non-survivor cannot hope to truly grasp. And yet this everyday language is precisely all the writer has at his or her disposal, as Levi says in another chapter of *Survival in Auschwitz*:

> Just as our hunger has nothing to do with the feeling of missing a meal, so our way of being cold has need of a special word. We say "hunger," we say "tiredness," "fear," and "pain," we say "winter," and they are different things. They are free words, created and used by free men who lived, in happiness and in suffering, in their homes. If the Lagers had lasted longer, a new, harsh language would have come into being; and we feel the need of this language in order to express what it means to labor all day in the wind, in temperatures below freezing, wearing only a shirt, underpants, a cloth jacket and trousers, and in our body weakness, hunger, and knowledge of the approaching end.[57]

Given Levi's magisterial knowledge and appreciation of great texts in the Western tradition, it is no wonder that he would turn to literary tropes as a way to expand the imagination of the reader, so that the depth of the experience he seeks to convey might be better understood.[58]

Second, if we look at the way in which this purported literary escape ultimately works in this chapter, a continuity *is* imaginable that is not at all deceptive. The tension created by Dante's text as interpreted by Levi has continued to build through the chapter. They have now arrived at the kitchen and Levi cites the following:

> Tre volte il fe' girar con tutte l'acque,
> Alla quarta levar la poppa in suso
> La prora ire in giu; come altrui piacque ...

> Three times it turned her round with all the waters; and at the fourth, it lifted up the stern so that our prow plunged deep, as pleased an Other ...

They are now standing in line for the soup. They hear the all-important announcement of its ingredients, in German, Italian, French, and Polish: cabbage and beets. The chapter ends dramatically, with the single line "Infin che 'l mar fu sopra noi rinchiuso" (Until the sea again closed – over us) that brings to a conclusion both the canto of Dante and the canto of Levi.[59]

The implication is that Levi, Jean, and all of their comrades are submerged, are about to drown along with Ulysses's crew, following Dante's version of the story of Ulysses. The end of Ulysses, drowned with his men after their fateful voyage, here works as a direct allegory for the submersion of these prisoners in Auschwitz, and so there is indeed continuity, and a very depressing one indeed.

Regarding the question of irony that Langer also raises, it seems clear that he intends it as the irony of believing that mental escape from the camp, even through Dante, is possible. It strikes me, however, that there is another irony at work here, the one operant in the notion that both Dante and Levi make their interlocutors "eager," with their speech:

> Li miei compagni fec'io si' acuti ... I spurred my comrades with this brief
> address to meet the journey with such eagerness ... and I try, but in vain,
> to explain how many things this "eagerness" means.[60]

Levi struggles with the translation of the word "acuti" (keen, eager): how to translate it, how to convey the eagerness it signifies, thus emphasizing the power of language to seduce. Listeners are made so eager that the eventual shipwreck, for Ulysses's men, or the submersion, for Levi and Jean, is that much more painful. The persuasion heard in Dante is that of Ulysses urging on his men: rhetorical seduction of the highest order, as it is precisely their worth, their potential as human beings, of which Ulysses reminds them. The crisis of the drowning is sometimes simply read as the moment in which the literary transcendence of Dante cedes to the brutal reality of the camp, but it seems apparent that it goes much further than this and that the two shipwrecks cannot ultimately be distinguished. Levi's project of teaching Italian to Jean is inextricably intertwined, thematically and linguistically, with Ulysses's rhetorical seduction of his men. And so irony here can also refer to the perils of rhetorical persuasion to be found in both texts. Perhaps the reader of Levi's text is not immune to this seduction either: in fact, this might go a long way in explaining the critical hagiography regarding the interpretation of Levi's use of Dante.

The appearance in the middle of Auschwitz of a great classical text in all of its rhetorical and aesthetic splendour, rather than being viewed as providing a "deceptive continuity," can be seen to provide a deceptive consolation, but one with serious repercussions. A world in which Dante can be spoken out loud is a world that perhaps is not so bad after all, and a survivor who can engage in the consolations of high literature is a survivor who is very much *compos mentis* despite his surroundings. By extension, the fragment of aesthetic pleasure that Dante's text affords

Levi, Jean, and Levi's reader reassures this reader that a civilized world can still exist, despite overwhelming evidence to the contrary.

As to the place of high literature in this real hell, Levi makes the following commentary in one long rush of breath as they arrive:

> I hold Pikolo back, it is vitally necessary and urgent that he listen, that he understand this "as pleased an Other" before it's too late; tomorrow he or I might be dead, or we might never see each other again, I must tell him, I must explain to him about the Middle Ages, about the so human and so necessary and yet unexpected anachronism, and something else, something gigantic that I myself have only just seen, in a flash of intuition, perhaps the reason for our fate, for our being here today.[61]

The anachronism that Levi mentions, as he says "so human and so necessary and yet unexpected," leads to the something gigantic, his intuition that he cannot reveal to us because he cannot reveal it to himself. What precisely is the nature of that anachronism that he so carefully modifies and the something gigantic that he senses? I would assert that the notion of anachronism as it is employed here functions as a reference to *traslatio*, the carrying over, passing down, of the empire of literature, but cast here as anachronistic, something no longer relevant, literally behind the times. And this would point to a crisis in the very idea of the value of the transmission of high culture.

If we return to the idea that Levi is rediscovering his fundamental humanity through citing Dante, then this is a discovery that results in an even greater loss. Levi gains the consolation of high literature fleetingly, only to make the loss, its disappearance in the shipwreck, that much more intense. The deception lies in thinking that this is reacquired humanity at all, or that he won't pay a price for it. The text of Dante held up as any kind of consolation becomes a miserable failure under these conditions. Levi and Jean suffer a rude reawakening at the end of this chapter, when the poverty of cabbages and beets and their always present hunger and danger of starvation collides with the image of a shipwreck in which the seas close up over them.

Thinking for a moment about the liminal states that Levi often comments on, and the price that one pays for changing moral codes that he discusses, some other questions regarding his use of high literature arise. In his essay entitled "Shame," published many years later in his collection *The Drowned and the Saved*, he says: "It is always costly to change one's moral code: every heretic, apostate, and dissident knows this. We are no longer able to judge our own or other people's behavior at that time – which was governed by the moral code of that time – on the basis of today's codes."[62] What about changing aesthetic codes or changing linguistic registers? Is there a price to be paid for those as well? Is the price that of reliability or transparency of testimony? In a different essay, Langer comments: "The Canto of Ulysses is a dramatic enactment of Levi's deepest fear in writing about Auschwitz: how literary strategies might threaten and tarnish one's credibility as a witness."[63]

And now we have, as we say in Italian, arrived at the sauce. I assert quite the opposite: rather than constituting a threat to his credibility, Levi's literary strategies in the end strengthen his text of witnessing, because these strategies allow him to metaphorically represent loss in an intensely profound manner, much deeper than mimetic language could afford the reader, who cannot possibly understand what "cold" and "hunger" mean in the context of Auschwitz. Levi's theory and practice of writing emerges from moments such as these in his work, moments when he leads us, like Jean, to understand that it is highly figural language such as Dante's that can allow a deeper access to the text of trauma. His identity as a survivor centres on the mandate of telling the story, a mandate that he posits as just as important as survival itself. But his authorial identity is concerned with something else: the task of telling the best story possible, narrating as an end in itself. When he brings a testimonial mandate and a dominant literary strategy together in one text, there are contradictions between what he says about writing and how he actually practises it. Yet when these two appear to collide, despite ensuing tensions, we see his best and most powerful writing.

A very different text in which he demonstrates his magisterial command of literary models is found in a science fiction tale of his, "Angelica farfalla" (Angelic Butterfly). His use of Dante in this story does not close down the debate through a potentially inappropriate referential system, but does the very opposite: the Dantean subtext opens up an acutely felt deliberation about ethics and science. The story also illustrates the further development of his writerly identity, as it demonstrates concerns that range from the best use of literary models to how to structure a fictional story about the Holocaust that engages questions of scientific complicity.

Science, Fiction, and Writing: *Mon maître, mon monstre*

After the publication of *Survival in Auschwitz* and *The Reawakening*, Levi turned his hand to a very different type of writing, science fiction. He published his first collection of these stories, entitled *Storie naturali* (Natural Stories), in 1966, to be followed by another collection, *Vizio di forma* (Vice of Form), in 1971.[64] Levi's science fiction holds a surprisingly liminal place in his opus. Sometimes neglected by critics and not widely known by the reading public, the science fiction gave Levi a different mode of expression for some of the most compelling and serious issues to be found anywhere in his work, and the stories are quite significant for the development of his writing persona. The genre allowed him a liberating free play in which he could explore topics ranging from poem-writing machines to animals. Many of the stories are humorous and light-hearted, but others take on very serious concerns.

One of the themes that he develops in this fiction is the relation between modern science and the Holocaust. Levi elaborates their connection in one tale in particular by adopting a discourse of monstrosity as a method of exploring and reading scientific epistemology and its relation to scientific ethics and politics. The story also demonstrates his ability to move between genres and authors to brilliantly craft a complicated argument about this science as well as about the role of high culture.[65]

Levi has framed *Storie naturali* in terms of the monstrous through his choice of an epigraph from Rabelais's Renaissance masterpiece *Gargantua*. The tremendous richness of his science fiction is forecast and framed by this epigraph, which is a fertile study in complications. The section that Levi abridges and cites is from the well-known fourth chapter, choosing the passage that comes directly after the description of Gargantua's strange birth from his mother's left ear:

> I don't care if you believe it, but an honest man, a man of good sense, always believes what he is told, and what he finds written down. Does not Solomon say, in Proverbs XIV, "The simple believeth every word, etc."? ... For my part I find nothing written in the Holy Bible which contradicts it. If this had been the will of God, would you say that He could not have performed it? For goodness' sake do not obfuscate our brains with such an idle thought. For I say to you that to God nothing is impossible. If it had been His will, women would have produced their children in that way, by ear, forever afterwards. Was not Bacchus begotten by Jupiter's thigh? ...

Was not Minerva born from Jupiter's brain by way of his ear? ... Castor and Pollux from the shell of an egg laid and hatched by Leda? But you would be even more flabbergasted if I were now to expound for you the whole chapter of Pliny in which he speaks of strange and unnatural births; and, anyhow, I am not such a barefaced liar as he was. Read chapter Three of the seventh book of his Natural History, and don't tease my brain any more on the subject.[66]

Once the reader has scanned this epigraph, Levi's own title, *Storie naturali* (Natural Stories), is no longer a mystery. But even though Levi reveals Pliny as the source for his title, the question of the epigraph is far from solved. One wonders, for example, why Levi doesn't just cite Pliny for the epigraph, since the title of his collection suggests that this may be a rewriting of or modelling after Pliny. Why the double frame, Rabelais citing Pliny? The differences between the works of Pliny and Rabelais are vast: the one a historical narrative that tries to convince through anecdotes, eyewitnessing, and claims to veracity and the other an ironic, enormous super-fiction that depends on hyperbole and exaggeration as its *modus operandi*. Seeking to undermine those truth claims on Pliny's part, Rabelais creates an ironic distancing from the subject of monstrous birth. He achieves this through the veiled hostility of jokes and obscenities, and through the epistemology and genealogy of lying that he presents, using Pliny as both his source and his scapegoat.

Rabelais, however, is anything but straightforward himself. He is emblematic of the author with many identities, as he was at once physician and priest, sceptic and believer, obscene and reverent. Levi names Rabelais as one of his literary influences in *A Search for Roots*, his homage to authors who most influenced him, and in an essay in *Other People's Trades* entitled "François Rabelais," Levi dubs him "mon maître," my master. Their affinities extend to the biographical: Rabelais was a practising physician turned writer and Levi a chemist turned writer. In discussing the complications of Rabelais's masterpiece *Gargantua*, Levi says: "Rabelais's very life, or at least what we know of it, is a tangle of contradictions, a whirlwind of activities apparently incompatible with one another, or with the image of the author that we traditionally reconstruct from his writings."[67]

Through the topic that Rabelais discusses in the above passage, which frames Levi's own text, Levi establishes the subject of the monstrous as central to his own stories, as it was to Rabelais. In the Rabelaisian passage, a strong connection is established between literary genealogies and monstrous generation, a thematic juxtaposition that will serve Levi's text well. The choice of Rabelais as both source of an epigraph and a literary and thematic model for monstrous childbirth carries with it the weight of Rabelais's own anxieties concerning literary genealogies and models. Carla Freccero, in her study *Father Figures: Genealogy and Narrative Structure in Rabelais*, asserts the following about these tensions: "a predicament of filial succession structures Rabelais's narrative, even as it constitutes the themes: of the writer as author of 'his' book, of the narrator as royal historiographer, of the son Pantagruel and his gigantic father Gargantua."[68] By citing the instance of Gargantua's birth in Rabelais's text, Levi is drawing upon the highly charged moment of the establishment of the dynasty Gargantua-Pantagruel, a moment that is intertwined with and dependent upon the thematic model provided by Pliny's text. Levi is entering into Rabelais's "predicament of filial succession" as well through this choice, as this epigraph is both constitutive of Levi's own themes and simultaneously undermines them through parody.

The questions raised by this epigraph are thus complex, as Levi is creating an ironic framing of his own text, perhaps going so far as to emulate Rabelais's elusiveness, declaring his own text to be lies. Is he setting up distinctions or, even worse, similarities between lying, or fiction, and the empirical world of science? Does this epigraph function as a technique for embracing contradictions that provides Levi with an equivocal approach to his own difficult, ambiguous topic? Even while he adopts and pluralizes Pliny's title, Levi rejects Pliny as his sole source for the topic of monstrous childbirth through his choice of Rabelais. Using Rabelais as a frame for his text furnishes a way for Levi to enter the world of science fiction, pure fantasy, the world of his own empiricism and Pliny's left behind, and offers him as well a model of the scientist turned writer. When the reader looks at the double theme of the Rabelaisian citation, it appears that both are relevant to Levi's text: the subject of monstrous birth, and Rabelais's formulation of the writer as liar, the potentially threatened and threatening believability of the story when there is no empirical proof. But unlike in Rabelais, many of the subjects that Levi chooses are not so far from a possible future reality, and he has declared his *storie* as multiple, in opposition to Pliny's singular History.

Levi's tale "Angelica farfalla" (Angelic Butterfly), found in *Storie naturali*, illustrates more precisely what is at stake in the double theme and the double frame of the epigraph by creating a scenario in which monstrous generation is achieved through the Nazification of science. The story also puts forth the role of literary and cultural genealogies as models in the propagation of the monstrous, and it demonstrates Levi's mastery in balancing ancient and modern texts as epistemological models for his tale of science gone awry.

Levi does not specify either the time period or the country in which the story takes place; he evokes the postwar period rather than stating it explicitly. Nonetheless, the place is easily identifiable as postwar Germany. A team of Allied researchers, consisting of a Frenchman, an American, a Russian, and an Englishman, go to a bombed-out neighbourhood to investigate a rumour about a grotesque medical experiment that supposedly took place there. The first line alludes to a lack of rapport between the researchers: "They sat in the Jeep stiff and silent: for two months they had shared the same quarters but still weren't on the friendliest terms."[69] This lack of ease or trust can be understood as referring to uncomfortable relations between the Allied countries at the end of the war, and also between members of the scientific community. The latter interpretation is strengthened when the reader learns on the next page that the group speaks German as their common language. Not only the language of the defeated oppressor, German is also a major language of the scientific community. What constitutes "community" is thrown into question by this apparent rupture in mutual comprehension. The story thus begins balanced between two poles of reference, one political and the other scientific. The use of German suggests an appropriation of the defeated genocidal culture, based on the exigencies of the political situation as well as those of the scientific community. It suggests as well the impossibility of truly moving away from either, as the rest of the story will demonstrate.

Levi has divided the story into two parts. The first details the political environment and lays out the scientific experiment, and the second deals with the events and repercussions resulting from the science. Four prisoners, whom the reader assumes are either Jewish or belong to another group singled out for extermination by the Nazis, have been victims of a experiment designed to imitate the axolotl, a salamander-like creature that lives in Mexican lakes. This creature is called an "intolerable heresy" as well as a "little monster" by the colonel who explains the experiment to the others, because of its uncanny ability to reproduce at the larval stage.[70] This ability, known as neoteny, obviates the need for the next stage in life. In other words, if a butterfly, for example, reproduces at the larval stage, why turn into a butterfly? The biological imperative of reproduction is bypassed by neoteny, thus rendering further stages of life superfluous. From the neoteny of the axolotl, Professor Leeb, the Nazi scientist who designed the experiment, concludes that other species may also be capable of neoteny. The colonel continues explaining Leeb's theories, found in a manuscript that Leeb has left behind, to the team of researchers:

> This condition may not be as exceptional as it seems, ... other animals, perhaps many, maybe all, maybe even mankind, have something in reserve, a potentiality, an ulterior capacity for development. Beyond all expectations, this capability is found in the early drafts, the bad drafts, and they can become "others," but they don't, only because death intervenes first. So, in conclusion, we, too, are neotenic.[71]

Leeb's theory claims that if the thyroid extracts of the axolotl are administered, a molting will take place before the death of the subject: in other words, it will turn the subject of the experiment into a creature with a potential second stage of life. His manuscript details the theoretical bases for the concept of neoteny, and states as well that he is carrying out some modest experimentation along these lines in a civilian dwelling, giving the address. After the war, the manuscript is found and it leads the team to the experiment and its remains:

> The floor was strewn with filthy rags, paper, bones, feathers, fruit peelings; using the blade of a knife, the American carefully collected samples from large reddish-brown stains and placed them in a glass tube. In one corner, a mound of unidentifiable material, white and gray, dry; it stank of ammonia and rotten eggs and was teeming with worms. "Herrenvolk!" said the Russian contemptuously (the language they spoke together was German).

When these samples are analysed, the colonel announces that he has found everything in them: "Everything's in there: blood, cement, cat piss, mouse piss, sauerkraut, beer – in other words, the quintessence of Germany."[72]

The remains found in the apartment allow the research team to attempt to reconstruct the experiment based on the physical evidence left behind. But that analysis, evidenced by the Russian's remark and the colonel's, is based on more than just an objective assessment of the facts. Due to the confusing hybrid nature of what they have found, their analysis must depend to some degree on their cultural/political assessment of the situation. The descriptions "Herrenvolk" and the "quintessence of Germany" reflect their analysis of the political agenda underlying the scientific one. Their disdainful comprehension of the political milieu in which these remains are found allows the colonel and the Russian to understand, while at the same time distancing themselves from, the tainted suspect nature of the remains as scientific artefacts. They are thus able to account for the fact that Nazi scientific ideology has polluted physical evidence to the point of creating mad hybrid mixtures. These remains are basically unreadable without the explanation afforded by Leeb's manuscript.

The research team finds a neighbour, Gertrude, who lived across from the apartment house where the experiment took place and who, at the end of the story, comes to the police station to tell her side of the events. In a structure mirroring that of a mystery, only after readers learn the scientific lesson of neoteny do they learn the fate of its victims, as Gertrude's testimony reveals:

"In September 1943, a military truck arrived: four men in uniform and four in street clothes got out. The civilians were all very thin and kept their heads lowered; there were two men and two women ... I was very curious, but my father kept saying, 'Let it go, don't concern yourself with what's going on in there. We Germans, the less we know, the better.' Then the bombings came; the house at No. 26 remained standing, but twice the blast caused the windows to shatter. The first time, I was able to see that the four people in the first-floor room were lying on straw mats on the floor. They were covered up, as if it were the middle of winter, though at the time it was exceptionally hot. They looked as if they were dead or sleeping ... the second time, both the straw mats and the people were gone. There were four horizontal poles at midheight on which four beasts were perched ... four birds: they looked like vultures, though I've only seen vultures in the movies. They were frightened and making a terrifying noise ... I couldn't see their heads very well because our windows were too high; but they were not very nice to look at and they made quite an impression ...Then the Russians came, and the end of the war, and everyone was hungry ... One night we saw a lot of people talking in the street in front of No. 26. Then someone opened the door and everyone went inside, pushing and shoving. I said to my father, 'I'm going to see what's happening.' He gave me the same little speech as before, but I was hungry and I went. When I got there it was already almost over." "What was over?" "They had killed them, with clubs and knives, and they had already chopped them to pieces."[73]

The last paragraph of the story ends with an account of the end of Leeb: the official version is that he is dead, a suicide, but the colonel does not believe this: he instead comments, "men like him give up only when they fail, and, however you judge this dirty business, he had succeeded."[74]

The manuscript that Leeb left behind provides a second source for the reconstruction of the scientific experiment, after the physical remains have been examined. Calling it "a very curious mixture of acute observations, rash generalizations, extravagant and obscure theories, literary and mythological digressions, polemical asides full of spite, and rampant adulation for Very Important People of the moment," the colonel recounts that the manuscript contains bizarre case histories as well as a chapter on "the iconography of angels and devils, from Sumeri to Melozzo of Forlí, and from Cimabue to Rouault."[75] The manuscript concludes that "angels are not fantastical inventions, or supernatural beings, or a poetic fantasy, but represent our future."[76]

The points of reference for Leeb's hybrid model for the experiment shift around in an interdisciplinary frenzy between religion, art, science, and history. By citing cultural and artistic monuments, Leeb endeavours to situate his own experiment within acceptable cultural bounds. To complete this attempted reconciliation of cultural history and his experiment, he cites Dante as a religious and cultural authority, as a justification and an inspiration. As epigraph to his manuscript, the colonel tells us, Leeb has used a citation from Dante's *Purgatory* 10, "which alludes to worms, insects that are far from perfection, and 'angelic butterflies.'"[77] This is the citation:

O superbi cristian, miseri lassi,
che, de la vista de la mente infermi,
fidanza avete ne' retrosi passi,
non v'accorgete voi che noi siam vermi
nati a formar l'angelica farfalla,
che vola a la giustizia sanza schermi?

Di che l'animo vostro in alto galla,
poi siete quasi antomata in difetto,
sì come vermo in cui formazion falla?

(O vainglorious Christians, miserable wretches!
Sick in the visions engendered in your minds
you put your trust in backward steps.
do you not see that we are born as worms
though able to transform to form into angelic butterflies
that unimpeded soar to justice?
What makes your mind rear up so high?
You are, as it were, defective creatures
like the unformed worm, shaped from the mud.)[78]

Through this framing of Leeb's manuscript, Levi provides us with yet another literary and theoretical reference for his story. The very title, "Angelica farfalla," refers to Leeb's epigraph, a relationship emphasized by Levi's capitalization of the word *farfalla* in his story. Like the Rabelaisian epigraph that sets the tone for the entire collection of stories, this framing plunges the text into further complications through its distortion of Dante. The appeal of Leeb's experiment is that this potential second stage of life is a greater one, a glorious one: downright angelic. Leeb deliberately misreads the Dante: aside from the more obvious problem of playing God that Leeb's experiment raises, at this moment in Purgatory, Dante is being given a lesson about humility and pride. Instead of understanding this message in Dante's text, Leeb has taken on the role of the creator, unproblematically embracing the very hubris that Dante's text calls into question.[79]

Leeb's misreading and misuse of Dante raises the issue of literary models already present in the Rabelaisian epigraph to Levi's collection of stories. Is Dante a pertinent literary model for this story, either in terms of Leeb's appropriation of Dante for his epigraph or in terms of our understanding of Levi's title to this story? Is it a question of repairing "defective" humankind here, when we speak of the Nazis' assessment of and "solution" to the issue of "inferior" racial groups? Leeb's experiment was certainly not aimed at fostering the spiritual well-being of his victims, but rather at using them to further experimental science. Theoretical science in the context of this story is hardly progressive or redemptive; it is homicidal, dark, and tortured. Leeb's Dante is an ethical model to which the world of this science cannot possibly aspire, yet Leeb clearly attempts to use it as a justification for his experiment.

Through the recounting of Leeb's manuscript and its Dantean framing, Levi produces a critique via which to evaluate the moral standing of the experiment. The most egregious sin that science commits here, through the figure of Leeb, is that of hubris: attempting to not only position itself next to art, next to high culture like that of Dante's, theological in nature and redemptive in intent, but to go so far as to create heavenly bodies as well.

Due to Leeb's prideful misreading, the Dante epigraph functions as more of a screen than a gloss on his activities, evoking a relevant piece of history as well as a model for inhumane medical experimentation. Once the historical background of the story is considered, its title suggests not Dante but instead the figure of Josef Mengele, nicknamed the "Angel of Death." Mengele was the infamous head physician of Auschwitz, one of the most nefarious physicians in the history of medicine. Chiefly responsible for deciding which people coming off the deportation trains would be killed immediately and which would work as slave labourers at Auschwitz until they perished, Mengele also oversaw and conducted inhumane medical experimentation at the camp, which usually resulted in the tortured death or permanent disfigurement of his victims. Nazi experiments were conducted under the pretext of furthering medical knowledge and research, and there have been debates up to the present day about the ethical implications of using the resulting data. As Levi's tale ends in the horrendous death of Leeb's victims, a far cry from divine perfection, these results are in fact much closer to what the name of Mengele evokes, as the story explores issues closely related to the reality of Nazi medical experimentation.

Levi provides a pessimistic ending to his story, as he suggests that Leeb may resurface: he, like Mengele, disappeared after the war, his fate unknown. Mengele hid in Paraguay and Bolivia, his existence an enigma, and finally died in 1979 from natural causes, still a free man. Only in 1986 was his identity definitively established. What Levi's narrator says about Leeb, and indirectly about Mengele, goes beyond the judgment of the acts of a single individual and is also applicable to the inhumane data and theories resulting from Nazi medicine. These data and theories are still in evidence, and still exist on the periphery of acceptable medical and ethical practice.[80]

Looking back now at the epigraph, we can see that Levi's choice of the subject of monstrous childbirth appears more relevant to the tale here told, although taken much more literally than in Rabelais's rendition. An understanding of the issues of maternity/paternity involved helps bridge the apparent gap between a fanciful and whimsical approach to monstrous generation and the all-too-serious one apparent in this story. The subject of monstrous childbirth that has Rabelais enthralled has been a major topos since Aristotle, and was of particular and rather obsessive interest during the Renaissance. In her study *Monstrous Imagination*, Marie- Hélène Huet states that

> a remarkably persistent line of thought argued that monstrous progeny resulted from the disorder of the maternal imagination. Instead of reproducing the father's image, as nature commands, the monstrous child bore witness to the violent desires that moved the mother at the time of conception or during pregnancy. The resulting offspring carried the marks of her whims and fancy rather than the recognizable features of its legitimate genitor. The monster thus erased paternity and proclaimed the dangerous power of the female imagination.[81]

Huet gives the example of a woman who purportedly looked too long at a portrait of the religious figure of St John the Baptist covered in furs and then gave birth to a hairy baby. The mother's undifferentiated blasphemous interpretation of the portrait is similar to the function that Leeb performs in Levi's story: Leeb takes the words of Dante, which represent theology, too literally as he attempts to mimic divine creation. Leeb's maternal relation to his monsters is a crucial piece of the equation. The victims are metamorphosed into monsters while hidden from public view. When their gestation is discovered, the unconcerned and hungry public destroys the products of conception through a semi-cannibalistic act. The status of this act as cannibalism is confused by the fact that the creatures are no longer fully recognizable as human beings; they are at least partially metamorphized into other creatures. Their heads, however, retain a semblance of masked human appearance, as Gertrude describes them: "They looked like the heads of mummies you see in museums."[82] The ambiguity regarding the cannibalism reflects the victims' ambiguous state as hybrid humans/monsters. The neighbours, as unconcerned bystanders during the war (to wit, Gertrude's father's statement "Let it go … We Germans, the less we know, the better") but willing consumers just afterwards, are caught up in this web of ambiguity. The situation reflects the complexity of the issues surrounding bystander passivity and complicity and their relation to active collaboration, a critically important issue for Levi that he engages elsewhere in his work.[83]

Leeb's maternal scientific imaginings in combination with his selective use of scientific knowledge have led to an exercise of unbridled scientific imagination. His attempt to transcend the human state to reach a higher plane has, like the Tower of Babel, failed as a catastrophe of hubris. But more than that, his experiment has involved unwilling human victims and thus participates fully in the dehumanization and Nazification of science during the Third Reich. Levi has evoked a scenario of medical experimentation in which the theory is as monstrous as the ultimately deformed subject or victims of the theory – in fact much more monstrous, as the victims of the theory remain innocent. Leeb functions as the mother of this grotesque childbirth, and so he shares in the essence of the monstrosity, as does his science. Monstrous childbirth is conceived in the epigraph to *Storie naturali*, but is borne and devoured only through the infelicitous combination of Nazi ideology and science.

In the introduction to *Monster Theory*, Joel Cohen has remarked that the monster always escapes.[84] The inevitability of the monster's escape, however, is in serious question in Levi's rendition, because the very identity of the monster shifts. Leeb has created monsters out of human beings, but Levi shows the real monster to be on the first level dehumanized science and on the second level those uncaring neighbours who are willing to eat the product of monstrous conception after turning a blind eye during the war to those same victims' fate. Has the monster really escaped, and what does "escape" mean in this context? The false monsters, the victims, have achieved a false escape as they have been consumed. But Leeb, the real monster of the tale, has disappeared, perhaps to practise monstrous science once again. As the colonel says about him, "I believe that if you searched for him, you would find him, and perhaps not too far away. I believe we haven't heard the last of Professor Leeb."[85]

The colonel's use of the conditional tense is highly suggestive. He does not suggest that the researchers should look thoroughly for Leeb, or that anyone will: he merely states that it would be possible to find him if anyone bothered to look. The idea that no one will do so is precisely the problem. The lack of commitment to ethical practices, lack of concern on the part of the populace, and government indifference have all ultimately resulted in Leeb's escape, suggesting as well that times have not really changed since the end of the war.

Levi sets this up as an admonition to those who would believe that history cannot repeat itself. It is not only the appearance of the monstrous that constitutes a problem. It is the resolution of the monstrous as well that demonstrates whether the underlying situation that created the monster is truly being confronted or, as in this case, merely disappears for the time being. Huet remarks that "several traditions linked the word 'monster' to the idea of showing or warning. One belief, following Augustine's *City of God*, held that the word 'monster' derived from the Latin *monstrare*: to show, to display."[86] The Augustinian tradition informs the Italian tradition, the one at the heart of Levi's concept of the relationship between *mostro* (monster) and *mostrare* (to show). The monster as warning, as demonstration of both the divine and the opposite of the divine, is highly relevant to Levi's tale of the marriage of bad politics to bad science. Monstrous science becomes one with the monstrosity of the Holocaust in Levi's reading, as he demonstrates their theoretical and practical relationship. The racialist scientific theory behind the Holocaust is the same theory that motivated, allowed, and encouraged medical experimentation on the prisoners.[87] The spectre of the millions of victims of the Holocaust, whose murders were committed largely through the application of chemistry and the medical experimentation of that same era, lies behind Levi's assessment of the dark potential of science in this story.

After one looks at the framing of Levi's tale within its historical context, it becomes even clearer that the story stands in antithesis to Dante and the world of potential redemption of his "angelic butterfly." High culture is held up as an impossibility, but that very impossibility has its own lesson to impart. The two epigraphs – Levi's Rabelaisian epigraph to his collection and, within a fictive framework, the Nazi scientist's appropriation of Dante – appear quite different from one another, as the distance between Dante and Rabelais is enormous. Perhaps the Rabelaisian model, however, of the first epigraph is not so very different after all from Levi's use of Dante in the second. In the Rabelaisian epigraph, the activity of narration is centred on lying, a perceived failure of the text to impart truth or to even try to do so; and Levi's use of Dante also underscores the notion of an elusive truth put into crisis. Ultimately Levi's story marginalizes Dante as not only irrelevant, but potentially misleading and dangerous: arrogant aspirations to becoming "angelic butterflies" have led to imprisonment, medical experiments, death, and finally a kind of cannibalism involving neighbours who have become complicitous in Leeb's crime. Levi has thoroughly undermined any desired ironic reading of his text, set up through the Rabelaisian epi-graph, by the sheer despondency of this *storia* only too *naturale*. In other words, in the sense of the potential harm that unethical science can do, there is no real lying possible, the excesses referred to by Rabelais and documented by Pliny are all too achievable, and we as readers bring this knowledge to our reading of Levi's text.

Levi effectively sets up a tension between the question of the believ-ability of events raised by Rabelais in the epigraph and the historical reality of the Holocaust. What sort of events are too horrible to be fully grasped? Those of fiction, represented by Rabelais who makes fun of Pliny's truth claims, or those crimes perpetrated by the Third Reich? What is at stake in our understanding of them? Levi's events lie some-where in a most problematic middle, and he demonstrates just how complicated that middle ground is. What he describes in "Angelica farfalla" is verisimilitude: neither wholly fictional, given the context, nor wholly believable, given the far-fetched scientific parameters of the experiment.

This situation leaves the science that created Levi's monstrosities in a highly ambiguous space. Is Levi, himself indebted to science in his long career as a chemist, launching a frontal attack on the morals and eth-ics of scientific experiment? Though this story appears to constitute a major critique of scientific ambition, Levi uses two strategies to under-mine understanding it as a critique of science.

The first is accomplished through Levi's framing of Leeb's manu-script. The colonel effectively marginalizes the science used in the experiment through his delineation of Leeb's sources for his experi-ment as misappropriations. The second strategy is a more complicated one: science, while still under fire, is isolated from a generalized cri-tique, because the experiment in question takes place under Nazism and is so extreme in nature. The political setting for the experiment tends to mask what is wrong with the science itself. Yet at the same time, the very context that weakens the scientific critique also strength-ens it: the harsh reality of the Nazi medical experiments that serve as a backdrop emphasizes the potential reality of what Levi describes, since the setting for the story is historical and not fictive. Levi has covered a lot of ground: from Rabelaisian irony about lying to Pliny's earnest anecdotes, from science so extreme that it situates itself as a creator of angels to the even-more-evil but very real Josef Mengele as the subtext to the Dante citation. Through his strategy of framing and contextual-izing, Levi effectively demonstrates that truth cannot or should not be harder to believe than fiction. Our understanding of the Third Reich as capable of anything further undermines the fictive nature of this story, and brings it closer to a depressing verisimilitude.

Levi's warning about the dangers of science in this tale comes through loud and clear, found even in the similarity of name between "Leeb" and "Levi." The immediate problem may disappear for the time being, just as Leeb has disappeared, but the seduction of scientific knowledge, and the potential abandonment of humane values and ethics, will always be there to tempt another practitioner, perhaps in another time and another place, and perhaps not so far away. Levi underscores the dangers of misreading and misunderstanding in the story itself, in the epigraph contained within Leeb's document, and finally in the Rabelaisian epigraph framing the entire collection of stories. This emphasis on misreading functions as a warning regarding our understanding of history and the tendency of history to repeat itself. Levi's indictment of science as potentially bloody and ruthless is historically tied to the Holocaust in this story, but at the same time he makes it clear that the monster of unethical science, and that of bigotry, is not specific or limited to the Holocaust but can return at any time.

His magisterial balancing of scientific ethics, diverse literary models, and fiction is a testament to the complex and highly nuanced writer's identity he has achieved at this middle point in his career. This balancing also demonstrates the depth of the connection between his scientific self and that of the writer.

What is particularly interesting, and significant regarding Levi's identity as a writer, is that Levi fleshes out these connections in his writerly practice, as demonstrated in this story. This stands apart from the *theory* of writing he discusses elsewhere, as his essays about the relation of chemistry to writing do not achieve the tremendous interdisciplinary depth of this science fiction tale, built on a bedrock of real questions still plaguing our world. Levi's avowed practice of writing and the brilliance of what he actually achieves do not, in other words, even come close to being the same, as he consistently undersells what he is able to accomplish. The first part of the story is thus how he achieves a writerly identity, and what it looks like. How this writerly identity, achieved through brilliant interdisciplinary and generic experimentation, interacts with autobiography, shame, and testimony is the next part of the story.

The next chapter will engage questions of the autobiographical mode. The beginnings of this discourse, as I've discussed, are found in his testimony, as Levi rejects an autobiographical mode in favour of a telling that represents other survivors as well. There are several of Levi's texts that directly engage the question of autobiography, including *The Periodic Table*, as well as demonstrating dramatic tensions and conflicts between the autobiographical mode and storytelling.

Chapter Four

Against Autobiography

Troubles overcome are good to tell.

From a Yiddish proverb, the consoling notion that *ibergekumene tsores iz gut tsu dertseylin*, troubles overcome are good to tell, appears as the epigraph to Levi's 1975 *The Periodic Table*. But as a counter, indeed perhaps a more accurate portrayal of the struggle of the survivor, Levi also frequently refers to Coleridge's "The Rime of the Ancient Mariner." In the end, this may provide a more appropriate trope because, as Jonathan Druker puts it, "the survivor often speaks, and then speaks again, precisely because his troubles will *not* be overcome."[1] The tension between these two very different sentiments – one that affirms the positive aspects of telling the story, the other its extreme pain, its *tsores* – expresses much of what is problematic for Levi about the telling of his life story. The how and when of that life story, the way in which it is necessarily bracketed within his identity as a survivor, leads to some contradictions and extreme positions within its articulation. These tensions become manifest at the end of *The Periodic Table*, his text that most closely resembles autobiography, although he firmly rejects that characterization, at least within the scope of the text itself.

The question of the most appropriate trope to represent the telling of the story parallels similar questions regarding the best genre to use in that telling. This chapter will explore some very different texts of Levi's to examine how he established his identity as a survivor within the exigencies of recounting his life story, and his decisions about which stories to present and precisely how to tell them. His identity as a survivor and as a writer emerges within the constraints of an autobiographical mode that he seems to find most problematic. The project of autobiography is often shuttled into the background in Levi's writing in order to make rhetorical space for the communal subject. In some of his texts, diverse strategies are employed to ensure that the autobiographical subject appears as secondary, as the vision of the world is foregrounded over a vision of the self. In Levi's work, the investigation of the self commonly found in autobiography is instead an exploration of the damage done to the self by the experience of the camp. Looking at the issue of auto-biography gives us access to important aspects of Levi's identity as a writer as well as to his testimonial project.

Generally speaking, the question of autobiography in Holocaust tes-timony needs to be examined with the effects of trauma in mind, as does the telling of the life story by a survivor in works not directly testimonial. Are the aims of autobiography different in this context? How do they play out within testimony, and what different kinds of questions are engendered? Is the label of autobiography even the right one to apply to these texts, or does the status of testimony automati-cally and insistently trump autobiography? To put it another way, can autobiography and testimony peacefully coexist in the same text, or do they work at odds with one another?

In *The Limits of Autobiography,* Leigh Gilmore raises the question of how trauma relates to autobiography and testimony. Her analysis of some central concerns helps elucidate what is at stake in Levi's writing regarding the telling of the life story. In her statements about what con-stitutes autobiography, Gilmore considers the following:

> Autobiography's project – to tell the story of one's life – appears to constrain self-representation through its almost legalistic definition of truth telling, its anxiety about invention, and its preference for the literal and verifiable, even in the presence of some ambivalence about those criteria. As a genre, autobiography is characterized less by a set of formal elements than by a rhetorical setting in which a person places herself or himself within testimonial contexts as seemingly diverse as the Christian confession, the scandalous memoirs of the rogue, and the coming-out story in order to achieve as proximate a relation as possible to what constitutes truth in that discourse.[2]

The concerns that Gilmore raises are pertinent to anxieties expressed in Levi's writing regarding the status of his work as testimonial and his use of figural language, as well as tensions about fictionalizing his story. The "testimonial context," as she calls it, is certainly present, yet in Holocaust testimony, or any testimony about trauma that goes beyond a single victim, this category must be nuanced quite differently than in other forms of autobiographical writing that primarily concern only the individual. The testimonial aspect of autobiography has as a principal function the lending of authority and credibility to the purported facts and events in the individual's life: in other words, an individual witnessing about a single subject. But in testimony that also involves an entire group, the weight and responsibility of the recounting of a larger picture is felt most strongly: many other lives, many other fates, and so the context is necessarily widened. Imagine, if you will, a Holocaust testimony that never mentions other prisoners and what happened to them, and this point becomes clear. Such a testimony does not and cannot exist.

Levi's "anxiety about invention" in *Survival in Auschwitz* comes out at the end of the preface, as he adds, "It seems to me unnecessary to add that none of the facts are invented."[3] His concern about the verifiable leads him to statements about his writing and his method that severely underplay the literariness of this writing and the consummate skill involved.

Gilmore discusses the pitfalls of the autobiographical mode in the context of recounting trauma:

> At the same time language about trauma is theorized as an impossibility, language is pressed forward as that which can heal the survivor of trauma. Thus language bears a heavy burden in the theorization of trauma. It marks a site where expectations amass both: can language be found for this experience? Will a listener emerge who can hear it? Attempts to meet these expectations generate incompatible assertions that both metaphorize and literalize trauma. For one example, to take one view, trauma cannot be spoken of or written about in any mode other than the literal. To do so risks negating it. In this construction, language may merely record trauma even as its figural properties in the speaker's imagination threatened to contaminate trauma's historical purity.[4]

The question of figural properties that Gilmore raises speaks to the tensions in Levi's work regarding the figures or tropes he uses to express the depth of the experience, addressed in the previous chapter. These issues also bring up another concern, that of the precise identity of the self that is recounting as well as the self being recounted.

Holocaust testimony in some respects shares characteristics with conversion narratives, those works that chart the development of the self from one stage to another through intense experience. It is typically the former self, such as Dante, St Augustine, or Rousseau, to name three well-known examples, who undergoes the voyage or journey, whether it be a literal journey or a spiritual one, and the new self that recounts both the liminal space in which the journey takes place and its resolution and ensuing change of identity. In Dante, this split between selves is an explicit theme of the text, expressed in the notion of Dante the pilgrim, the Dante undergoing the spiritual journey, versus Dante the poet, the figure who writes about it and is thematized within the text.

Sharon Portnoff, in her research on the relationship between Levi and the great epic poets Homer, Virgil, and Dante, has remarked, "Each of these epics, even as it establishes or perpetuates the tradition of writing epic poems, itself questions the adequacy of this form in conveying human experience. Just so, Levi writes his memoir in a way that both attests to his Holocaust experience and also questions the adequacy of his formulation."[5] She discusses the ways in which Levi interacts with Dante's poem that bring to light crises in Holocaust witnessing, namely, the difficulty of the juxtaposition of reality and the imagination. She points out the ways in which Levi refers to the epic journey by his choice of names for chapters:

> By titling his first chapter "The Journey," and by alluding at the *beginning* of his second chapter "On the Bottom" – where he arrives at the camp – to a moment toward the *end* of Dante's *Inferno* – the moment when the pilgrim encounters Satan himself and finds himself neither dead nor alive – Levi points to what cannot be spoken: all that follows in the next fifteen chapters of the book; that is, the brute fact of being "on the other side" of human existence and on the other side of human experience and of stories about that experience. This pointing to what is omitted at the beginning of the memoir is reinforced at its end: by titling his last chapter "The *Story* of Ten Days" (emphasis added), Levi reintroduces story-telling, suggesting that, as experience and formulation of experience begin to separate themselves again, the ability to only point to one's mortality and to tell stories returns.[6]

Portnoff's formulation leads one to wonder if in his testimonial works Levi's form of autobiography can be separated from his use of the model of the epic journey. But in the end is this then another way of deflecting autobiography, or rewriting the form to suit his needs? The journey itself, as in Dante, takes on as much if not more importance than its outcome, which is the emergence of the new self.

Levi wrote three major texts that recount his life story to varying degrees: *Survival in Auschwitz*, *The Reawakening*, and *The Periodic Table* are all reflections on his life, as well as his poetry, which also closely echoes his life experiences. The three texts are very different in nature; the first is largely testimonial, the second testimonial as well as a picaresque tale, and the third the story of his vocation. The last two are openly fictionalized, and *The Periodic Table* effectively theorizes fictionalizing within the genre of autobiography. Autobiography as the centre of the narrative is in general deflected in Levi's work, shunted aside in favour of group witnessing, as discussed in the previous chapter, in favour of telling a good tale, and in favour of a wide range of other narrative strategies found in *The Periodic Table*.

As shown in my discussion of the construction of Levi's writerly identity, Levi makes clear his preference for the plural pronoun in *Survival in Auschwitz*, for writing that is able to represent not just an individual but the entire community. This preference extends itself to these other texts as well, in the form of a displacement of the autobiographical self, and in fact this tendency emerges as a pattern in Levi's writing. Before we look at the details of those texts, it's crucial to understand what's at stake for Levi in the telling of his story: how does the autobiographical mode intersect with the testimonial, and what are the consequences of this intersection? This query needs to be examined from several points of view: the perceived reliability of the testimony insofar as it is able to convey historical fact, the image of the self that is constructed, and finally, the model of conversion narrative that is created through the text. I first examine the ways in which Levi constructs his narrating self in *The Reawakening* and then look at how he deconstructs this narrating self in *The Periodic Table*. Finally, I consider his poem written late in life, "The Survivor," which exemplifies the intersection between the narrating self and the shame that imbues the identity of the survivor, resulting in an autobiographical mode that is vexed and all but impossible.

The Identity of a Survivor

From his testimony recounting his time in Auschwitz, Levi moves to a different kind of memoir/testimony, *The Reawakening*, published in 1963. The Italian title for this text is *La tregua*, or "The Truce," changed by American publishers despite Levi's protests. Just how inappropriate this new title is becomes clear when the themes of the book are examined.

Levi made the following comments about its composition:

> I had told a story – why not tell another? The bug of writing had got into my blood. And so *The Truce* was born, where I told of my return from Auschwitz. In the first book I had paid attention to things; I wrote the second one fully aware that I could transmit experiences, but with a single aim: to write clearly in order to seek out contact with the public.[7]

Levi had clearly gained confidence from the success of the first book, and it is intriguing to see how that confidence expresses itself in his goal regarding writing as clear communication. But what he does not address here or anywhere else, except defensively, are the fictionalizing elements found in *The Reawakening*, changes that were noted by some fellow survivors, most vocally by Lello Perugia, the real-life basis for the character Cesare. Ian Thomson includes in his biography a letter that Levi sent to Lello apologizing for the fictionalizing:

> Honestly, I've been meaning to send you the book for some time, but I hesitated somewhat because one of the characters has got something to do with you. I feared you might be annoyed. You must be the judge of that. But please remember: (1), the words and adventures which I attribute to Cesare have been liberally recreated, interpreted, and, in part, invented; (2), in the opinion of all the readers I've spoken to, and all the critics of the newspapers up until now, this Cesare (who knows why?) ends up being quite a genial character.[8]

Levi's defensive letter to Lello is carefully constructed to placate him (which it evidently did not). The logic in Levi's letter reads as follows: the character of Cesare bears some resemblance to you, but readers and critics like the character, so what's the harm? His rhetorical question "who knows why?" regarding how well the character has turned out is quite charming: it is as if his creation of Cesare has nothing to do with his skill and is almost a matter of blind luck.

Levi's open admission of re-creation and invention raises some important issues. How fictionalizing can be used to tell a good story is self-evident; what is less obvious is how the inventions and recreations that Levi mentions fit into the texts' avowed goal of testimony or of its autobiographical function. *The Reawakening* is thus crucial for its contribution to an understanding of Levi's life story and how he chooses to write it, as well as for its portrayal of the liminal state of the survivor.

Once out of the concentration camp, Levi begins increasingly to use the singular pronoun *I* as he leaves the scene of trauma and goes back to a more civilized world. Told much in the vein of a picaresque novel from the third chapter until almost the end, the text recounts Levi's long and meandering way back to Italy after Soviet troops opened the gates of Auschwitz in January 1945. Embodying both of the narrative extremes Levi expresses, the text begins with painful chapters while still in Auschwitz, moves to happier and more liberated times whose recounting seems to bring him some joy, but is then bracketed at the end with an image of the permanently tortured survivor.

The first two chapters of *The Reawakening* present some of the most powerful writing found in Levi's opus, as well as further exploring the painful state of the survivor. In the first chapter, Levi examines the liminal state in which they find themselves after the arrival of the Russians. Entitled "The Thaw," it investigates the notion of thawing not only from the metereological point of view, in which winter is ending and the deep freeze of Polish winter melting, but as a softening of the state of captivity, of being slaves under the Nazis. The thaw itself is dangerous: with it, the camp turns into a "squalid bog" as the extremely unsanitary conditions make the very air a threat. The ill continue to die, and Levi himself continues to worsen. He makes clear as well the perils of the unfreezing of identity, as they pass from prisoner to a different state but are not yet free in any sense of the word.

Levi recounts a poignant moment with one of the others, a privileged German political prisoner, viewed with disgust by the general prisoners as part of the establishment. Weeping, in the middle of the night Thylle asks if Levi is awake, and they share an intense conversation: "It wasn't easy to make myself understood by him, not only for reasons of language but also because the thoughts that lay in our breasts on that long night were endless, marvelous, terrible, and above all confused."[9] Thylle, after he stops crying over his lost ten years of imprisonment, begins to sing the socialist theme, the "Internationale," leaving Levi "disturbed, distrustful, and moved." It is clear from this moment that the walls of the lager have come down not only physically but across symbolic distances. Thylle seeks to regain his old identity through the song, and through his conversation with a Jewish prisoner with whom he would not have had much contact, and certainly not friendly contact, before. The two explore a common liminal ground as they both examine their new state, which is post-prisoner but not yet post-lager. The system of the camp under the Nazis has disappeared, but no new order has yet appeared to take its place. *The Reawakening* explores what it means to be without a clear system, without barriers, without even a nation, as the former prisoners are taken from camp to camp within various Soviet territories and treated to a variety of different orders and systems. These changes often occurred without an apparent logic, as the former prisoners never knew what or when the next stage in their repatriation would be. Their re-establishment of an identity after dehumanization was equally in limbo.

The second chapter of *The Rewakening* contains the heart-wrenching story of Hurbinek, the three-year-old child who is literally and figurally deformed by his time in the camp, rendered speechless and incapable of communication. Despite the others' attempts to teach him language and save him both physically and emotionally, he perishes, and Levi writes about him, "Hurbinek died in early March 1945, free but not redeemed. Nothing remains of him: he bears witness through these words of mine."[10] In a very powerful way, Hurbinek stands in relationship to the rest of the ill survivors as they do to their own re-entry after the war. The need for language to express themselves, to be understood, the force of anguish: Hurbinek represents a microcosm of that survivor condition that depends on language and the ability to communicate, and with him it is shown to fail miserably.[11]

At the end of the passage on Hurbinek, Levi makes an enigmatic but important statement about Hurbinek's condition at his death: what precisely is meant by "free but not redeemed"? Furthermore, what does it mean to set up these terms in binary opposition? The translation is exact: the Italian original reads "libero ma non redento." The Latin root of the word "redeemed" opens up an epistemological itinerary, as a heavily commercial and transactional sense lies at the heart of the word: *Re*, again, and *emere*, to buy, to buy back, to buy again. "Redeemed" has also taken on a theological meaning, appearing in the Bible as the image of the Lord redeeming the Jews from Egypt, getting them out of slavery, saving them from the hands of a tyrant; it then passes into the New Testament as a central tenet of Christianity. Yet there is a paralysing irony present in Levi's use of the term "redeemed": no divine redemption of any of the prisoners took place. They were not, after all, freed from the land of Egypt and the hand of the tyrant, but rather "freed" by the act of the Russians opening the gates of Auschwitz as they discovered the camp and its remaining inhabitants. What that freedom could and did mean to the former prisoners, limited and limiting as it was, becomes one of the central themes of *The Reawakening*.

The notion of redemption has also been applied, most problematically, to a broader concept of the Holocaust as carrying theological implications. From this viewpoint, the suffering purportedly served a higher cause, an approach that makes martyrs out of the victims. Levi speaks strongly against this view in his essay "The Gray Zone," stating, "It is disingenuous, absurd, and historically false to argue that a hellish system such as National Socialism sanctifies its victims.[12] In using Hurbinek as an example of the limitations of freedom, Levi directly opposes this kind of appropriation. Hurbinek may have been free, but only in the technical sense that Auschwitz was no longer under Nazi domination: freedom understood as release from slavery. Levi sets up the term "free" in opposition to the higher meaning of redemption, and so freedom as a concept is found lacking, found to be insufficient. Hurbinek's freedom, in the face of a lack of redemption, was in the end meaningless. What is also important about the story of Hurbinek, however, is the way in which it functions as an interpretative key for the text in general and for the issues that permeate Levi's other works. This fiercely stated opposition of "freedom" and "redemption" speaks directly to the issue of survivor identity that Levi explores deeply in this text.

One of the main framing devices that Levi employs in *The Reawakening* is the epigraphic poem "Wstawac" (Reveille) that posits the inexorability and circularity of the survivor's condition. Levi uses dream sequences as well as poetry to further investigate this state:

Sognavamo nelle notti feroci
Sogni densi e violenti
Sognati con anima e corpo
Tornare; mangiare; raccontare.
Finché suonava breve sommesso
Il commando dell'alba:
"Wstawac":
E si spezzava in petto il cuore.
Ora abbiamo ritrovato la casa
Il nostro ventre é sazio,
Abbiamo finito di raccontare.

E tempo. Presto udremo ancora
Il commando straniero:
"Wstawac"

We dreamed in the fierce nights
Dreams dense and violent
Dreamt with body and soul
Return, eat, tell the story.
Until the soft short command
at dawn:
"Wstawac"
And the heart would break in our breast
Now we have found our homes, again.
Our bellies are full.
We have finished telling the story.
It's time. Soon we will hear again the foreign command,
"Wstawac."[13]

Speaking to the inexorable nature of the camp, the poem contains the sentiment that although "we have finished telling the story," the moment arrives and the "foreign command" will be heard once more. But even more crucial is the radical notion that the telling of the stories is not, in the end, liberating, or even that important in the grand scheme of things. That camp reveille *will* be heard again, despite freedom, despite having told the story. The limbo in which they find themselves can be a painful and repetitive place, as Levi signals to us through this epigraphic poem.

Levi employs dreams as the ideal liminal state in which the survivors' past lives and future lives meld together, in a set of activities that are presented as if they are equally weighted, equally important: returning, eating, and telling the story of the imprisonment and genocide. Physical survival, through the preservation of the body by sustenance, segues directly to narrating, as if telling the story is a naturalized consequence of survival. But is the narration ultimately enough? Through this poem, Levi challenges his own avowals regarding the importance of writing and how it saved him after his return. He puts into crisis what survival ultimately means and can mean.

Portnoff discusses the relationship of Dante's *Purgatory* to "Reveille," in light of the painful state of limbo and what it entails, as she explores Levi's narrative challenge, stated as: "How does one continue the fight with the knowledge that one's vigilance will fail, that the terms of the fight are those things aspired to and not, perhaps, those things that are? And further, is it beneficial to human experience to continue to define the fight in these terms?" Portnoff concludes her argument by declaring what the transformation of experience to art can mean for Levi: "Echoing Dante, Levi, by the act of writing the poem, affirms the possibility of the transformative value of art. And also, like Dante, Levi communicates to his more attentive readers that this transformative value is ambiguous: his dramatization may reflect only those things aspired to, not those things that are."[14] The relationship of personal experience to the art of talking about it is central in this text, and demonstrates the anguish of the tale as well as that of the teller. The challenge of autobiography for Levi thus stands squarely in the middle of a negotiation between his own experience and the way he chooses to develop his literary identity.

The change of self that Levi's experience of the camp has engendered is nowhere more apparent than in *The Reawakening*. In that text, unlike conventional conversion narratives in which the focus is on a binary opposition of the old self to the new self, a third stage is apparent in which the self that has been damaged by the experience struggles to establish an identity. One could argue that in more conventional conversion narratives there is also a third stage present, that of the self undergoing the experience, but I contend that there is a substantial difference between a figure such as Dante undergoing change as a part of the poetic experience and the traumatized self of the survivor. The survivor always bears a part of that agonistic struggle in the new self, and not just in memory, whereas the fully converted self of a conversion narrative is just that: the ideological power of the conversion narrative depends on the full ceding of the old self to the new self.

Levi frames *The Reawakening* with dreams that resemble nightmares: the end of *The Reawakening* also contains the dream of being at home. The dream functions as a gloss for the epigraphic poem, as it repeats the themes of the inescapability of the camp, even in freedom:

> It's a dream within another dream, varying in its details, unique in its substance. I am at the table with my family, or friends, or at work, or in a verdant countryside – in a serene, relaxed setting, in other words, apparently without tension and pain – and yet I feel a subtle, profound anguish, the definite sensation of a looming threat. And in fact, as the dream proceeds, little by little or brutally, each time in a different way, everything

collapses and is destroyed around me, the scene, the walls, the people, and the anguish becomes more intense and more precise. Everything has now turned into chaos; I am alone at the center of a gray and murky void, and, yes, I know what this means, and I also know that I have always known it. I am again in the Lager, and nothing outside the Lager was true. The rest was a brief holiday, or a trick of the senses, a dream: the family, nature in flower, the house. Now this internal dream, the dream of peace, is over, and in the external dream, which continues coldly, I hear the sound of a well-known voice: a single word, not imperious, but brief and subdued. It is the dawn command of Auschwitz, a foreign word, feared and expected: get up, "Wstawac."[15]

Elspeth Probyn affirms that "the geography of affect that Levi creates moves from out to in, and the freedom of the outside is always enfolded in the terror of the camp."[16] I would add that the permanence of the lager condition is evoked in his very choice of language, his referring to it as a dream (*sogno*) rather than a nightmare (*incubo*). The word "nightmare," which he could well have chosen instead, would have cast the content as separate, farther from his everyday reality, a distancing strategy. Instead, this dream is part of his everyday life, and the language he uses to describe it reflects this state. The appropriateness of the original title of the work becomes clear: the *truce*, essentially a liminal state, is emphasized through this bracketing of a purported freedom that only exists theoretically. The survivor is revealed as entirely unable to escape what has happened, both in dreams and in waking. The American title *The Reawakening* here shows its utter inappropriateness: Levi's theme in the text is not a "reawakening," which would imply healing, perhaps a fresh start, but rather the notion that the damaged state of the survivor is a permanent one and that at best only a truce of this status can be called.

The contrast with the dreams recounted in *Survival in Auschwitz* is noteworthy. In that text, the dreams describe the suffocating feeling not only of being in the camp, but of returning home to discover that no one wants to hear the story: a dream that Levi tells us was shared by other prisoners, which adds to that text's functioning as the witnessing for a group:

Here is my sister, with some unidentifiable friends of mine and many other people. They are all listening to me and it is this very story that I am telling … It is an intense pleasure, physical, inexpressible, to be at home, among friendly people, and to have so many things to recount, but I can't help noticing that my listeners do not follow me. In fact, they are completely indifferent: they speak confusedly among themselves of other things, as if I were not there. My sister looks at me, gets up, and goes away without a word ... My dream stands before me, still warm, and although I'm awake I'm filled with its anguish. And then I remember that it's not just any dream, and that since I arrived here I have dreamed it not once but many times, with hardly any variations in setting or details. I am now fully awake and I remember that I recounted it to Alberto and that he confided, to my amazement, that it's also his dream and the dream of many others, perhaps of everyone. Why does it happen? Why is the pain of every day so constantly translated, in our dreams, into the ever repeated scene of the story told and not listened to?[17]

The intense pain of the dream in *Survival in Auschwitz* is the threat of not being listened to, of not finding an interlocutor or an audience to hear the stories of trauma. In *The Reawakening*, the audience has indeed been found, the stories told, and yet this doesn't make a difference in the condition of the survivor. Moreover, it speaks directly against the consoling notion, furthered by Levi himself, that writing, telling the story, served as a kind of healing for the survivor. What kind of healing is actually possible in the scenario that Levi draws for us in the epigraphic poem "Wstavac" and at the end of *The Reawakening*, his text of returning home? It is important to note that *The Reawakening* was written more than fifteen years after *Survival in Auschwitz*, and the reader may well infer that Levi's thought has changed regarding the usefulness of writing to alleviate the condition of the survivor.

If writing as the failed alleviation of pain is a central message of *The Reawakening*, the text that ostensibly sought to re-establish his identity after the *lager*, how does that notion affect the telling of his life story in other texts, written later in his career? *The Periodic Table*, very different from his testimonial texts in subject and in writing style, tells an intriguing and dissimilar story of how Levi viewed autobiography.

The Periodic Table: Against Autobiography[18]

First published in 1975, *The Periodic Table* is a text in which many of the tensions and conflicts regarding Levi's self-conception and self-presentation as an author come to light, due at least in part to the hybrid nature of the text itself. Generic considerations are confounded from the start by this text. It is to some degree a testimony, if we consider the episode in the transit camp and the one that takes place in Auschwitz. It has the flavour of a *Bildungsroman* in the early chapters in which Levi explores his scientific vocation in school, and it contains wildly imaginative stories that Levi wrote before and after deportation. There are episodes that follow the simultaneous events of the war and Levi's marginalization from the Italian mainstream, post-Holocaust chapters that engage themes of Holocaust denial and of the role of Levi's chemistry in the war, and tales that focus upon his life at work. Levi sternly disavows the notion that *The Periodic Table* also belongs to the genre of autobiography, but nonetheless tensions abound regarding the presence of an autobiographical mode in the work.

His changing of factual details in some of the chapters of *The Periodic Table* points precisely in this direction, that Levi was much more interested in being a writer's writer than he was willing to openly acknowledge. In this text, the exigencies of narrative, of telling a powerful story, are more important than the exigencies of fact. The two chapters that most powerfully explore these tensions are the first and the last, the framing texts: "Argon" and "Carbon." The conflicts within them go far beyond the parameters of generic hybridism and diversity of topic. These two tales work in conjunction to illustrate the dominance of the narrator, the telling of the tale, over the representation of the autobiographical self.

Levi makes some intriguing pronouncements about autobiography in the introduction to "Carbon," as he discusses the textual status of *The Periodic Table* as a whole. He states what this book is not, as if he needed, at the very end of the text, some disclaimers:

> This is not a chemistry treatise: my presumption does not reach so far, "ma voix est foible, et même un peu profane." Nor is it an autobiography, except in the partial and symbolic limits within which every piece of writing – in fact every human work – is an autobiography.[19]

Perhaps trying to avoid the appearance of self-indulgence, Levi continues by situating his text in a much broader perspective. Breaking the text out of the realm of the individual self, which he perhaps sees as constricting, hedonistic, or worse, he universalizes it not only for other chemists but for "everyone":

> It is, or would have liked to be, a micro-history, the history of an occupation and its defeats, victories, and sufferings, such as everyone wishes to

recount when he feels close to the end of the arc of his career, and art ceases to be long.[20]

"Carbon" is framed so as to deflect autobiography by reducing it to a matter-of-fact condition to which "any piece of writing" is subject. Levi finishes his framing by reducing the author to a biological condition that appears to exclude conscious thought or control in the culmination of the text. And yet, in an interview in 1975 after *The Periodic Table* came out, Levi was asked point blank if the book is the autobiography of a chemist. Levi replied, "In a certain sense, yes, but any book which only has one face, that you can only read in one way, is, I think, a rather poor book. A good book is necessarily, I won't say ambiguous, but at least polyvalent."[21] Levi thus opens up his text to the possibility of multiple readings and makes more room for autobiography in the interview than he does within the text itself.

The question of autobiography within *The Periodic Table*, indeed, is not easily dispatched. The majority of the chapters recount specific events that happened to Levi in his life as a chemist. The poetic and metaphoric shaping of each tale, the philosophical and ethical musings in which Levi engages, and finally the obvious autobiographical foundation of the text can only underscore the presence of self, not lead to the erasure of same that Levi posits as a *fait accompli* at the end of "Carbon." His tales complicate his reluctant and unwilling autobiographical project.

The first chapter of *The Periodic Table*, "Argon," as discussed in chapter 2, also has a lot to say about the autobiographical project, even in the way it fictionalizes the family story. The relationship of autobiography to genealogy appears ambiguously transparent, as the self begins, is thus grounded, in family history. Levi's deflection of who constituted his actual family into the larger community in most of "Argon" reflects a similar logic found in the last tale of "Carbon," as the author as subject disappears into his topic. "Argon" and "Carbon" thus share a strategy of containment of the autobiographical through its displacement.

A useful way of looking at Levi's shift from family to community and what is at stake in this transformation is found in the critical distinctions drawn by Pierre Nora between history and memory. Nora writes that the two can be distinguished by their differing roles: the first, history, creates *lieux de mémoire*, sites of memory; the second, memory, *milieux de mémoire*, environs of memory. Memory is defined as that which takes place within a community or a group, a living tradition that needs no historical documentation for future generations' memory. The presence of institutionalized history is antithetical to memory conceived in this way:

> Memory and history, far from being synonymous, appear now to be in fundamental opposition … [memory] remains in permanent evolution, open to the dialectic of remembering and forgetting, unconscious of its successive deformations, vulnerable to manipulation and appropriation … Memory is a perpetually active phenomenon, a bond tying us to the eternal present; history is a representation of the past. Memory … only accommodates those facts that suit it; it nourishes recollections that may be out of focus or telescopic.[22]

Nora's distinctions are useful here to the extent that they elucidate Levi's shift from what he calls "history" to a more accurate description of his text found in Nora's concept of memory. Levi's anecdotes in "Argon," insofar as they shun both historical and genealogical accuracy, take on the qualities of a mythic oral tradition. In the light of Levi's actual family history, the stories recounted in "Argon" follow closely Nora's predictions of how memory functions, as they "accommodate only those facts that suit it."

Shunning autobiography in favour of what he claims is "microhistory," Levi's rendition of "family" history turns out to be ahistorical, mythical, and grounded in transmitted memory rather than in fact. The memory environment that he creates in "Argon" is antithetical to both factually based history and personal autobiography. The narrative milieu that Levi creates does far more than deny autobiography or tease it out from between the lines. The very constructions that he depends on to avoid autobiography – fictive genealogy, denial of family history in favour of "cognates" that really are false in the end – create the fiction that, *alla lunga*, in the long run, reveals the most.

The question of authority in the text and that of the text is directly relevant to central questions of witnessing and of the role of Holocaust commemoration in Levi's writing. In what ways is the narrating self found in "Argon" and in "Carbon" conditioned or even dictated by the demands of commemoration? What is the relationship between Levi's stance on autobiography and his other writing imperatives, namely testimony and witnessing? Massimo Lollini argues convincingly that

> Levi's autobiographical perspective is focused on a subject inextricably open to the presence of another, the shame and guilt of being alive in the

place of another ... Levi's works help us appreciate the subject's position in auto-biographical text which is different than that conceived by traditional notions of autobiography. Levi forces us to discover a subject whose memory is driven not by personal remembrance but by the death of the other.[23]

Lollini cites the chapter entitled "Iron" and its story of Sandro Delmastro, whom Levi commemorates at the end, as an example of the conflation of the goals of autobiography and commemoration. Levi ends the chapter on his friend Sandro, murdered by the fascists, with these words:

> Today I know it's hopeless to try to clothe a man in words, make him live again on the written page, especially a man like Sandro. He was not a man to talk about, or build monuments to, he who laughed at monuments: he was all in his actions, and when those ended nothing of him remained, nothing except words, precisely.[24]

Levi openly expresses his frustration with written words as his only commemorative tool, similar to his statement regarding Hurbinek: "Nothing remains of him: he bears witness through these words of mine."[25] Yet between these two texts there is a development in Levi's thought about the ability of language to commemorate: Levi implies that his words about Hurbinek do serve a useful function, whereas in the case of Sandro language cannot properly reflect the essence of the person commemorated.

Lollini's points regarding the motivations of Levi's writing are well taken. If we think of Levi's text as being imbued with the need to commemorate, his self-erasure becomes a strategy to highlight commemoration. But Levi attributes part of the failure of commemorative language in Sandro's case – "especially a man like Sandro" – to the fact that Sandro was a man of action who laughed at monuments. The attitude of the commemorated one towards commemoration itself is quite beside the point: commemoration, like funereal rites, is meant for the survivors, not for the dead.

A crucial intertextual moment occurs at the end of *The Periodic Table* that focuses on the role of the poetic voice in both establishing and abolishing narrative authority. Levi cites Voltaire in the first paragraph of "Carbon": "This is not a chemistry treatise: my presumption does not reach so far, 'ma voix est foible, et même un peu profane.'[26] The citation is taken from the second line of Voltaire's satirical epic poem on Joan of Arc, entitled "La Pucelle D'Orleans" (The Serving Girl of Orleans), begun in 1730. The first three lines of the poem are:

Vous m'ordonnez de célébrer des saints
Ma voix est faible, et même un peu profane.
Il faut pourtant vous chanter cette Jeanne

You command me to celebrate the saints,
But my voice is weak and also a little profane.
Yet it is necessary to sing to you of this Joan.[27]

Levi's citation of Voltaire introduces "Carbon" in a highly enigmatic fashion, and it works retroactively, along with the rest of his disclaimers already discussed, to define and condition *The Periodic Table* just as the reader arrives at the last chapter of that text. Voltaire's introduction to his poem mocks the conventional disclaimer regarding the unworthiness of the poet, a voice that Levi adopts as his own through this citation. Usually, however, the convention stops with the poet's modesty and is not extended to the profane. Yet if we think about Voltaire's poem to follow, the profane makes sense: secular, satirical, viciously mocking the notion of Joan of Arc's purity, the poem reduces the debate about Joan's saintliness to a debate about her virginity, a question that is definitively settled when she has an affair within the narrative. The profane moves from the initial disclaimer to becoming the expression of the poetic voice.

Levi simultaneously disavows the poetic nature of his text by casting his own poetic voice as weak and profane while at the same time embracing the literariness of the text through this citation from a well-known eighteenth-century author. He continues to frame the end of his text within the parameters of high culture through a transformative partial citation of Horace: *ars longa vita brevis* becomes "l'arte cessa di essere lunga," art ceases to be long lasting. There is a resonance as well with Levi's use of the expression *alla lunga* in "Argon," in the long run. How long the run actually is appears to be in crisis, in both instances.

The Horace citation is invoked in "Carbon" just as Levi makes his move of denying *The Periodic Table* as autobiography through the dislocation onto the notion of "everyone" reaching the end of his or her career. As this end approaches, the logical assumption is that it is *vita* that is even more *brevis*, but instead Levi displaces the brevity of life unto art. In Horace, art stands in temporal opposition to life: art is long lasting while life is fleet. To render art as ceasing to be long lasting is a reversal of Horace's terms. Even more, it strongly suggests that the art dies with the poet; that it has, in the end, *alla lunga*, no lasting effect.

This reversal functions as a double reflection on the nature of art and autobiography and their relation for Levi. Levi's reversal comments on the quality of the art of the poet, substantiating the citation from Voltaire. It also speaks to what we might call Levi's theory of autobiography. For Levi, autobiography must take place through a displaced poetic voice: it can never be direct, it must pass through a series of filters and displacements. Its claim to authority comes from this very displacement. As Levi rejects the text as autobiography, he embraces the role of the poet – but he also ironically undermines it.

Levi leaves us with a set of reversals at the end of *The Periodic Table*, just as he demonstrates precisely how long his art is and will continue to be. He openly reduces and then rejects autobiography, only to reclaim it in the form of a displaced poetic voice that he celebrates and simultaneously undermines. His attempted removal of self from the text only leads to a stronger poetic voice, which he cannot successfully shake off onto a fictive and nostalgic notion of history. The attempted displacement onto "micro-history" in the end ultimately underlines the creativity of his voice.

"The Survivor" and the Anguish of the Mariner

Levi's own words, found in *La ricerca delle radici* (*A Search for Roots*), in the chapter on the influence that Conrad's "Youth" had upon him, perhaps illustrate best of all his relationship to the self and to telling the story of the self:

> Marlow appears here for the first time, his alter ego, and the narration is attributed to him. The reasons for this doubling are deep; I believe that the principle reason is Conrad's reserve: Marlow, so similar to him, frees him from the anguish of saying "I."[28]

This anguish, expressed through the trope of Conrad and his double, is nowhere more apparent than in a stunning poem Levi published in February 1984, towards the end of his life, in which he creates an alter ego through which to express the pain of surviving. The reasons for this pain reside in the strain of the telling, the duality of the self, as well as the nature of the audience that receives the tale.

"The Survivor" begins with a line in English from "The Ancient Mariner," so as to make no mistake about the origin of the literary reference. That the poem alludes to the mariner is not left to the reader's imagination, and the next lines are virtually indistinguishable from the poem except in subject. But how relevant and appropriate the theme of the mariner actually is needs to be examined in some detail.

The poem comprises two distinct sections. The first part describes a survivor, a generic survivor, recounted in the third person. In the second part, the survivor speaks but his speech, addressed to the ghosts who haunt him, is bracketed between quotation marks.

"Since then, at an uncertain hour,"
Dopo di allora, ad ora incerta,
Quella pena ritorna,
E se non trova chi lo ascolti
Gli brucia in petto il cuore.
Rivede i visi dei suoi compagni
Lividi nella prima luce,
Grigi di polvere di cemento,
Indistinti per nebbia,
Tinti di morte nei sonni inquieti:
A notte menano le mascelle
Sotto la mora greve dei sogni
Masticando una rapa che non c'è.
"Indietro, via di qui, gente sommersa,
Andate. Non ho soppiantato nessuno,
Non ho usurpato il pane di nessuno,
Nessuno è morto in vece mia. Nessuno.
Ritornate alla vostra nebbia.
Non è mia colpa se vivo e respiro
E mangio e bevo e dormo e vesto panni."

Since then, at an uncertain hour,"
That pain returns,
And if he does not find someone to listen
His heart burns in his chest
He sees again the faces of his companions
Pale in first light
Grey from cement dust,
Indistinct in the fog,

Shaded by death in restless sleep
At night they work their jaws
In the oppressive weight of dreams
Chewing a turnip that isn't there.
"Stand back, away from here, submerged people,
Go away. I haven't supplanted anyone,
Haven't usurped anyone's bread.
No one died in my place. No one.
Go back into your fog.
It's not my fault if I live and breathe,
And eat and drink and sleep and put on clothes."[29]

Dramatizing a split between Levi the narrator and Levi the survivor, Levi the writer begins by describing this generic survivor, and the necessity of telling his story: namely, the price that he will pay if he can't find an audience. The poem is complicated both in tone and in technique. There is a grammatical ambiguity to the Italian, as the "gli brucia in petto il cuore" of the original can also mean that the unavailable listener, the lack of an audience, is what burns his heart, rather than the untold story.

The model of the ancient mariner for Levi and his survivor's tale sets forth some particular interpretive challenges. The first few lines of Levi's poem are a paraphrasing of the end of Coleridge's poem:

Since then, at an uncertain hour,
That agony returns:
And till my ghastly tale is told,
This heart within me burns.

The ancient mariner has been cursed by his decision to shoot the albatross, an act that appears to have dire consequences for his shipmates as their fortunes become jinxed and the ship lies fallow. Two spirits are aroused by the shipmates' glee over the death of the albatross, and gamble for their souls: one spirit, named Death, takes the lives of the mariner's shipmates, but another, named Life in Death, wins a roll of the dice and takes that of the mariner himself. In order to expiate his sin, the mariner must tell his tale to a chosen audience:

I pass, like night, from land to land;
I have strange power of speech;
That moment that his face I see,

I know the man that must hear me:
To him my tale I teach.

There are elements that correspond strongly with Levi's feelings about his cursed state as a survivor: "life in death," left behind to tell the tale, he can only wander looking for the right audience, one that will pass down the message, as the end of his poem "Shemà" dictates. "Life" is thus dependent on narrating the tale of survival with its accompanying moral lessons. But the truly curious part of his adoption of the ancient mariner lies in the reason for guilt and survivor shame. What could be Levi's albatross besides survival itself? He did not choose his fate, as the mariner did by his senseless slaughter of the albatross. Lina Insana calls the image of the ancient mariner a "template for the surviving witness," as she states that "it is fitting that Levi chooses this interplay between dreaming and waking to articulate the same notion of divergent realities that motivates the Coleridge poem."[30] The realities for Levi, however, are not divergent, but have collapsed into a single entity.

Some interpretations of the poem look at it as a working out or a negotiation between the two realms, those of the spiritual world and the physical world. Perhaps Levi's mariner is trying to work out the differences between the world of the camp and the world of civilized society. He returns from the deep, as does the mariner: returns from a world little understood and never before navigated.[31]

The complicity of the mariner's shipmates is a curious aspect of the poem, as they initially condemn the mariner for shooting the bird and then rather randomly change their mind and defend his actions:

For all averred, I had killed the bird
That made the breeze to blow.
Ah wretch! said they, the bird to slay,
That made the breeze to blow!
Nor dim nor red, like God's own head,
The glorious Sun uprist:
Then all averred, I had killed the bird
That brought the fog and mist.
'Twas right, said they, such birds to slay,
That bring the fog and mist.[32]

As Coleridge's own gloss to the poem states, "But when the fog cleared off, they justify the same, and thus make themselves accomplices in the crime."[33] Another point of correspondence between the two works lies in the construction of the audience or reader. The wedding guest may beat his breast and complain, but he has no choice but to listen, which causes him to miss the wedding of his next of kin entirely. Tragedy is more important than celebration, and more can be learned from it, as he arises the next day wiser from hearing the tale. As I discussed in chapter 2, Levi's preoccupation with his potential reader is most clearly articulated in his poem "Shemà," in which he curses those who refuse to pass on the collective memory of the Shoah to their children:

> Or may your house fall apart,
> May illness impede you,
> May your children turn their faces from you.

The two also have in common the theme of departure and return; both share characteristics of conversion narratives, with the former self going through the experience and the new self living to narrate about it. In addition, the poem contains two references to Dante, and as is common in Levi's work, these references allow a deep exploration of themes. The first occurs in the subject's vision of his tormented companions in their restless sleep, "la mora greve," oppressive weight, which alludes to Dante's *Purgatory* 3, "la grave mora." *Mora* used for weight or stone is an archaic use of the term, and Levi knew Dante well enough to be paraphrasing him here. The occurrence concerns Manfred, who is in Purgatory because of his excommunication by the popes at the time, who didn't like his political allegiance with the Saracens. In Dante, the "grave mora" refers to Manfred's burial under weighty stones, as a reflection of his excommunicated state; his bones are found there, he tells Dante. His undignified burial can be read as Levi's commentary on the fate of Holocaust victims lacking a proper burial, thrown out as it were, like Manfred: "sotto la guardia della grave mora" (under the guard of the heavy weight) (Dante, *Purg.* 3, 127–9). The play on *grave/greve* is powerful in this context: the one connoting a physical heaviness, the other an emotional one.

In the second part of the poem, the survivor addresses these companions, presumed dead, as he exhorts them to return to the fog, a reference to the night and fog of Hitler's plan to eliminate resistance to the Nazi regime. "Nacht und Nebel" (Night and Fog) was the name given to a decree of 7 December 1941, issued by Hitler and signed by Field

Marshall Wilhelm Keitel, chief of the German Armed Forces High Command (Oberkommando der Wehrmacht, or OKW). The decree directed that persons in occupied territories engaging in activities intended to undermine the security of German troops were, upon capture, to be brought to Germany "by night and fog" for trial by special courts, thus circumventing military procedure and various conventions governing the treatment of prisoners.[34]

At the end of the poem, survivor shame hangs heavily in the air, as the survivor attempts to get these shades to leave him alone, and insists, perhaps too much, that he is not alive in the place of another. Is he trying to convince himself? But these ghosts won't leave him in peace, and he cannot forget. Levi makes it clear that peace does not exist for the survivor because of the murdered others, always present, at the outskirts of consciousness. Shame and witnessing are inextricably linked, and so the dead witnesses, the "real ones" as he says, come back to haunt the author who seeks to witness and to testify.

In the disturbing end to the poem Dante is evoked once more, as Levi cites "and eat and drink and sleep and put on clothes." This direct quotation is from the *Inferno*, canto 33, where the traitors are found deep in hell. This particular part of the canto is situated in the third zone of Ptolomea, in which those who betrayed their guests are found. Dante has just encountered one such, Branca Doria, whom he knew to be still alive on earth. He asks and is informed that after the great sin of treachery, a demon can possess the soul of a betrayer and cast it into hell, but the body remains on earth: "e mangia e bee e dorme e veste panni," and eats and drinks and sleeps and puts on clothes:

> "Sappie che, tosto che l'anima trade
> come fec' ïo, il corpo suo l'è tolto
> da un demonio, che poscia il governa
> mentre che 'l tempo suo tutto sia vòlto.
> Ella ruina in sì fatta cisterna;
> e forse pare ancor lo corpo suso
> de l'ombra che di qua dietro mi verna.
> Tu 'l dei saper, se tu vien pur mo giuso:
> elli è ser Branca Doria, e son più anni
> poscia passati ch'el fu sì racchiuso."
> "Io credo," diss' io lui, "che tu m'inganni;
> ché Branca Doria non morì unquanche,
> e mangia e bee e dorme e veste panni."

"Know that the moment when a soul betrays
as I did, its body is taken by a devil,
who has it then in his control
until the time allotted it has run.
The soul falls headlong to this cesspool.
Perhaps the body of this shade, who spends
the winter with me here, still walks the earth,
as you must know, if you've come down just now.
He is Branca d'Oria. Quite some years
have passed since he was thus confined."
"I think," I said to him, "you're fooling me.
For Branca d'Oria is not yet dead: he eats
and drinks and sleeps and puts on clothes."[35]

The Dantean borrowing casts the last lines of Levi's poem into very dark territory indeed. By citing this canto, Levi portrays this survivor as a betrayer of his companions, his soul in hell but his body still on earth: an incomplete survival, a survival at a terrible cost. In one of the grimmest moments in Levi's writing, he has gone well beyond the survivor shame that he so disturbingly outlines for us in his essay of the same name. Here he offers the reader an even more problematic view of the state of the survivor. Dante's Branca d'Oria was a Ghibelline nobleman who invited his father-in-law to a banquet in order to have him murdered. His soul was immediately cast down to hell by a demon while his living body, soulless, continued to walk the earth. This canto includes others who betrayed their guests, such as Fra Alberigo, who informs Dante of their sorry state. The notion of hospitality used for murder is a very grave sin indeed in Dante's world, but what is the connection to the state of the survivor?[36] Does Levi really mean to imply that surviving involves a betrayal of others of this magnitude? Or, despite the intensely negative connotations of this passage, could he quite simply not resist its drama, its ability to evoke the crisis of surviving while simultaneously suggesting the impossibility of that very survival?

Survival in this poem signifies a betrayal that implies the very loss of one's soul while the physical body still wanders the earth. Autobiography, as the story of an individual, becomes highly vexed, if not impossible, within these parameters. Autobiography is a narrative mode that is presumed to take place within civilized society. The text of trauma interferes with autobiography's aim of establishing the narration of an autonomous individual self. How Levi negotiates telling his life story within the parameters of trauma involves moments of extreme intensity. These negotiations are often tense and sometimes contradictory, but offer us a way into understanding the dilemma of the narrating survivor, as well as further understanding the constraints of Levi's writerly identity.

What lies so heavily in the text of "The Survivor" is Levi's exploration of what surviving means in the context of guilt and shame. Is it inevitably tied to a betrayal of those who died? Is survival in any real sense even possible within the terms that Levi lays out in this poem? The topic of shame in Levi's work is a difficult and heavy burden to bear, even for the reader; clearly that much more so for the author himself. In the next chapter I investigate the articulation of shame, and its relation to Levi's opus.

Chapter Five

Shame's Identity

Let each judge, on the basis of the picture outlined and the examples given above, how much of our ordinary moral world could survive on this side of the barbed wire.[1]

Levi's statements on witnessing and on testimony have been held up as critical models, as guideposts that can lead the reader through more traditional as well as postmodern discussions of what constitutes witnessing and testimony and how they function within the Holocaust narrative. They are cited widely throughout Holocaust and trauma studies; in fact, Levi's influence in this area and in others cannot be underestimated. He wrote about these two topics in many places in his opus, starting with *Survival in Auschwitz* and continuing throughout his forty-year career as a writer and philosopher of the Shoah.

Coupled with his discussion of testimony and of witnessing is a highly vexed concept of shame. Levi frequently raises this topic in his writings: it appears to be a concern central to his thought and to his very identity both as a writer and as a survivor. Towards the end of his life, he analyses it thoroughly and quite disturbingly in an essay entitled "Vergogna" (Shame)" published in his 1986 landmark collection *The Drowned and the Saved*. As the phenomenon of shame is a concern strongly linked both to survivor identity and to the giving of testimony, any discussion of his views on witnessing and testimony must also take into account his polemical views on this topic. Levi himself, as we shall see, directly links testimony to shame through his articulation on the most appropriate witnesses of the Shoah. These remarks regarding what he calls the "true witnesses" of the Shoah, namely the victims who perished, who did not survive to bear witness, have caused shock waves throughout both his general readership and the field of Holocaust studies. All the same his analysis, however disturbing, functions as an integral part of his thought on testimony: what constitutes that testimony, who furnishes its best voice.

Ruth Leys, in her outstanding study *After Auschwitz*, states that for the critic Giorgio Agamben "the experience of shame is also the experience of testimony."[2] I maintain that in many respects this statement is also true for Primo Levi, and makes the study of shame essential for the critic and reader of his work. In this chapter, I examine Levi's development of the concept of shame and how it relates to his testimony and to his identity as a survivor. His shame identity is best explored not only through looking at his statements on guilt and shame as well as critical analyses of these concepts, but also through examining how he represents shame through his figuration of the *Muselmänner*, those prisoners unable to survive the camp system. Levi's shame identity stands with his narrative voice. It comes through most distinctly at select moments that I will highlight, responding to certain narrative moments, and as such cannot be separated from either his writerly identity or from the autobiographical project.

There are three areas that bear exploration in the context of Levi and shame. The first is what shame means in the context of Holocaust testimony, the second what Levi himself says about it, and the third is the two figures he uses to represent it: the *Muselmänner* and the Medusa. It is in these figural representations that the tensions regarding the poetic expression of testimony and what those can mean in the context of survival are most clear.

Shame and the Holocaust Text

The topic of shame presents one of the most contentious aspects of any consideration of survivor testimonies. What shame means to the survivor, to the reader, to the society that allowed the massacre to happen, has been the topic of much painful discussion and reflection. Furthermore, shame's articulation in Holocaust writings has met with very strong reactions. These range from incredulity on the part of the reading public, that any survivor could bear the burden of guilt for atrocities beyond their control and could feel guilty for their own survival, to outrage that a society that could debase people to this degree would also allow them to bear a burden of shame.

Shame is a phenomenon that involves more than the individual. It extends in several different directions: it involves the survivor or victim, as the almost non-human remains to which he/she has been reduced, and it includes us and our blush of shame as we gaze upon the reduced figure through testimony about him/her. Shame implicates the witness to it as well as the society that produced atrocity.

Levi, unlike many other survivors, does not focus primarily on survivor guilt, but rather on a concept of shame that he develops within his opus. The differences between shame and guilt are crucially different in their effect upon the identity of the survivor. As David Shapiro remarks, "Guilt is concerned with what one does; shame has to do with what one is,"[3] and Ruth Leys comments:

> By common agreement, guilt concerns your actions, that is, what you do ... Shame, however, is held to concern not your actions but who you are, that is, your deficiencies and inadequacies as a person as these are revealed to the shaming gaze of the other, a shift of focus from actions to the self that makes the question of personal identity of paramount importance.[4]

To posit shame rather than guilt in the survivor is thus to place into question any overt culpability for actions leading to survival, but in its stead the very identity of the survivor is altered. It is this enduring change of identity that is the most devastating aspect of shame for the survivor. On the occasions when Levi uses the word "guilt," he is referring to actions, not to identity. When he uses the word "shame," it has far broader implications.

In reviewing the major debates over the past few years regarding the movement from guilt to shame as a focus of study, Leys makes a compelling argument for what's at stake in current critical discussions of shame in its relation to trauma and to Holocaust testimony, discussing the shift from what she calls the "'moral' concept of guilt in favour of the ethically different or 'freer' concept of shame"[5] and distinguishing between mimetic and antimimetic types of shame.[6] She attributes to Levi antimimesis, as he maintains a critical distance from what has happened to him, whereas the mimetic approach more generally involves identification with the perpetrator, a concept that Levi discusses in his essay on the gray zone in *The Drowned and the Saved*.

The rejection of shame or guilt as a condition of the survivor reveals some of the inherent tensions apparent in the discussions about this topic. In his groundbreaking work on Holocaust testimonies, Lawrence Langer rejects the notion of survivor guilt, as Leys says,

> not only because he thinks it deflects blame from the real culprits onto the victims themselves, but more generally because it belongs to what he regards as a normalizing, therapeutic, redemptive approach to the misery of the Holocaust that estranges us from the ultimately incomprehensible and unredeemable reality of the camps.[7]

Langer tries to contain shame, or even remove it entirely from the discussion, through the way he argues his case. Yet this approach, while admirable in its desire to spare the victim this second, devastating desubjectification, is not relevant if two conditions are present: the survivor has internalized a shame identity and has articulated this identity in their testimony. At the same time, Langer's overt resistance to shame is useful in that he makes us understand what is ethically objectionable about attaching shame to the victim, when shame's more appropriate object is the society that generated the dehumanization. Who "owns" the shame generated by the Shoah: the survivor? the society?

As Elie Wiesel remarks in his essay "A Plea for the Dead," written after the trial of Adolf Eichmann in the early 1960s: "the future frightens us, the past fills us with shame."[8] There is a deliberate ambiguity in Wiesel's statement regarding who constitutes the shamed "us" that speaks eloquently to the question of who is shamed by the Shoah: is it the witness, as Levi would maintain, or is it also everyone who comes into contact with it, including the human society that allowed it to happen, as Wiesel strongly suggests?

The psychologist David Shapiro offers insight into the reasons behind the owning of shame by the survivor:

> When Levi speaks of the irrationality of shame in this connection, he is speaking of people who of their own choice have done little or nothing to be ashamed of, but on the contrary have suffered the shameful acts of others. It is true that they have been forced to endure experiences or perform actions that in themselves might be considered shameful. But, in Levi's phrase, "on a rational plane" the fact that these actions were coerced and were in no way carried out at their own initiative might be thought to obviate shame. Not at all. It seems that the very condition of subjugation has the opposite effect; it intensifies or adds to feelings of shame. In other words, it is not only the experiences these people were forced to endure

or the actions they were forced to perform but their very helplessness and inability to resist that is reason for shame. It is the fact of subjugation itself that is damaging to self-respect.[9]

Levi's own typology of shame is multifaceted. As Sergio Parussa puts it, Levi goes from an articulation of "shame felt due to an actual transgression, to shame felt in the absence of evident transgression, from shame as a form of guilt to shame as consciousness of the existence of evil."[10] In order to more fully understand this, it's necessary to look carefully at different moments in his opus when the issue of shame is raised, and to pay particular attention to his use of the term "guilt" as opposed to that of "shame." He uses the word "guilt" in the essay on memory in *The Drowned and the Saved*, as he discusses the desire of the Nazis to shift onto the victim "the burden of guilt."[11] In the essay "Shame," he returns to this argument:

> Many people (and I myself) felt "shame" – that is, a sense of guilt – both during and after imprisonment, as numerous witnesses have verified and confirmed. Absurd though this may sound, it exists. I will try to interpret this phenomenon and to comment on the interpretations of others.[12]

Critics have taken these statements as proof that Levi interchanged the use of the two terms, but I believe instead that Levi is proposing a theory of shame and how it works, in which he deliberately begins with guilt and ends with shame. By putting the term "shame" in quotation marks, Levi is framing it as a specific notion that he is about to develop. The "sense of guilt" is the beginning of the phenomenon he will describe, not a synonym for it. This is quite apparent in the way in which he argues the case of suicide among survivors in the essay. At the beginning of the argument, Levi repeatedly uses the word "guilt":

> Suicide arises from a feeling of guilt that no punishment has come to alleviate … Why did we feel guilty? Once everything was over, the awareness dawned on us that we had done nothing, or not enough, against the system into which we had been absorbed.[13]

At the end of this discussion, however, he goes back to the word "shame": "So at the rational level there would not have been much to be ashamed of, but still the shame remained."[14] Guilt is used to indicate actions, or lack thereof: shame is the feeling that persists, that goes beyond the temporality of actions, and is the condition that deeply affects the soul of the survivor.

The two most fruitful ways of exploring the full ramifications of Levi's discourse on shame are through his development of shame throughout his opus and through his portrayal of the figure of shame, the *Muselmann*. This figure organizes a repository for shame in Levi's work, and contains as well a critique of witnessing and of testimony that constitutes a major paradox within Levi's work. But first it is important to further explore what Levi has to say about shame and how he frames his discourse about it.

From "The Gray Zone" to Shame: The *Muselmänner*

Levi's 1986 collection of essays *I sommersi e i salvati*, *The Drowned and The Saved*, more properly translated as the "Submerged and the Saved," contain his mature thoughts on the Shoah from a distance of forty years. It is here that we find his essay entitled "Shame," but we find also his landmark work "The Gray Zone," which has had a tremendous impact not only in Holocaust studies but in other studies of trauma as well, as it is widely cited and discussed. The way in which Levi constructed this book of essays is important, as it demonstrates connections between his chosen themes.

He begins with a preface, in which he states that

> the story of the Lagers has been written almost exclusively by people who, like me, did not plumb the depths. The ones who did never returned, or if they did their capacity for observation was paralyzed by pain and incomprehension.[15]

This is a statement he will make three times: once here, once in the essay entitled "The Gray Zone," and once in "Shame." Privileged prisoners had a better observatory, higher up, but according to Levi it was also falsified by the fact of their privilege. He also discusses the cowardice of the Germans in keeping the secret of the lagers: "Without this cowardice, the worst excesses would not have happened, and Europe and the world would be a different place today."[16] The entire set of essays can be seen as an extended conversation about shame, beginning with who can tell the story and who was keeping the secrets that allowed atrocity to continue, and ending with letters from Germans that make up the last chapter.

"The Gray Zone" directly precedes the essay on shame in *The Drowned and The Saved*, and for good reason. "The Gray Zone" articulates the difficulty of passing judgment on survivors, and discusses how many different paths, some tainted with the stench of collaboration, were open to those attempting to survive. His argument is nuanced and subtle, and places the reader in a better position to understand the even more difficult essay to follow, on shame. The essay challenges the reader to put themselves in the shoes of the victim, as he begins with a question: "Have we survivors succeeded in understanding and making other people understand our experience?"[17] From there, Levi launches a discussion of how "understand" can mean "simplify," affirming that simplification is necessary in our complicated world, but that the danger resides in the belief that simplification is reality. He draws this concept as one that pertains in particular to the camps, to a world in which there existed a gray zone of collaboration. The essay in its subtleties and nuances provides a comprehensive argument regarding collaboration from minor to major, but it also compels the reader to comprehend the inappropriateness of drawing black-and-white distinctions, while simultaneously pointing out that readers cannot really understand what it was like in the camps, because of the complexity of the moral situation and the desperate desire to survive that drove the inmates.

The essay ends with a plea to suspend judgment in the case of the ghetto leader Chaim Rumkowski, by asking how many of us today could have resisted the influences that drove him to collaboration:

> But there are extenuating circumstances: an infernal system, such as National Socialism, exercises a shocking power of corruption from which it is hard to shield oneself. It degrades its victims and assimilates them, because it requires major and minor complicity. You need a solid moral backbone to resist it, and Chaim Rumkowski, merchant of Lodz, together with his entire generation, had only a frail one at his disposal. But are we Europeans today any stronger? How would any of us behave if we were to be driven by necessity and at the same time tempted by something seductive?[18]

Levi makes a strong case not only for cutting Rumkowski a lot of moral slack, but for extending that latitude to the other inmates. He is persuasive in his arguments and eminently fair to those who could be seen as collaborators, such as the *Sonderkommando*: the prisoners ordered to run the crematoria, almost always Jewish, forced to move and despoil the corpses, selected for this duty and then periodically purged so that witnesses to the massacres would be few. For them, resistance meant immediate death.

Levi's articulations regarding the corruption of power, the degradation of the prisoners, the inevitability of the search for privilege so as to avoid starvation, results in a very compelling anti-shame argument that functions as a clear contextualization of the shame discussion to follow, that makes it clear where real responsibility for atrocities lies. The placement of this essay, in which an understanding of and empathy for the gray zone is developed as Levi absolves those who tried to survive by any means possible, is certainly not coincidental,.

Levi's full engagement with the topic of shame and with the *Muselmänner* comes in the essay that directly follows "The Gray Zone." "Shame," written towards the end of his life, begins with a citation from Leopardi and this famous poet's articulation of pleasure as the child of affliction. Levi, however, affirms that the legacy of pain is quite different: pain is the child of pain, a statement that Leopardi's binary opposition of pain to pleasure has broken down in the face of real trauma. He then problematically asserts that the real witnesses of the Shoah are all dead:

> Let me repeat that we, the survivors, are not the true witnesses. This is a troublesome notion that I became aware of gradually by reading other people's memoirs and rereading my own years later. We survivors are an anomalous and negligible minority. We are the ones who, because of our transgressions, ability, or luck, did not touch bottom. The ones who did, who saw the Gorgon, did not come back to tell, or they came back mute. But it is they, the "Muselmänner," the drowned, the witnesses to everything – they are the ones whose testimony would have had a comprehensive meaning. They are the rule, we are the exception.[19]

An examination of Levi's treatment of the figure of the *Muselmann* is essential in understanding his concept of shame. As Joseph Farrell has noted, "The *Muselmann* is a figure of reproach, an inadequate, pathetic figure who has failed."[20] In many respects, Levi's testimony about Auschwitz is enormously concerned with the *Muselmann* and how to deal with this figure. I am proposing the centrality of the figure of the *Muselmann* to Levi's thought, for two reasons. First, Levi adopts and even promotes this figure as a repository for shame, as I will demonstrate. And second, what can well be called a culture of hostility towards the *Muselmänner* is developed in Levi's works. This animus ultimately takes the form of a transference of shame onto this figure, as a close textual analysis of Levi's emergent thought on the topic will show. Levi is not alone in this attitude towards the *Muselmänner*: other survivors also write about them in a desubjectifying manner.[21] As Levi describes the *Muselmänner* in *Survival in Auschwitz*:

> And, in any case, it's clear that they are only passing through here, that in a few weeks nothing will remain of them but a handful of ashes in some nearby field and a checked-off number in a register. Although engulfed and swept along unceasingly by the innumerable crowd of those like them, they suffer and drag themselves on in an opaque inner solitude, and in solitude they die or disappear, leaving no trace in anyone's memory.[22]

The original Italian title of Levi's testimony, *If This Is a Man*, raises the question of what happened to humankind in Auschwitz: how far the dehumanization went, what its effects were, how it was implemented. The figure that came to represent the extremes of dehumanization is what the other prisoners called the *Muselmann*, "Muslim" in German. The origin of the term has been broadly discussed,[23] but it generally signified those prisoners who had from all appearances given up the struggle for survival and were waiting for their inevitable death.[24] Survivor and writer Giuliana Tedeschi provides a graphic and compelling description of their state:

> Malnourished bodies walking painfully on their legs, bodies literally reduced to skeletons, on which the skin sagged terribly, bodies infested all over with boils ... The soul seemed slowly to be leaving these neglected (*relitti*) bodies, abandoning the place that nature gives the body ... Here the body was observed declaring its misery, justifying with disgust and abomination its demise in the crematorium."[25]

The self-reflectiveness of Tedeschi's description, in which the physical body acts as a protagonist separate from its soul, raises compelling issues regarding who and what functions as the witness of the destruction, a question that Levi himself will raise and that has also been the focus of critical inquiry by Agamben, as will be discussed below. Zdzislaw Ryn and Stanilsaw Klodzinski describe stages of becoming *Muselmänner* that have as their physiological basis the progressive effects of malnutrition. In their view, the state of the *Muselmänner* is an overwhelmingly physical condition whose psychological dimensions are dictated by starvation.[26]

Manuela Consonni points out that survivors almost never describe themselves as former *Muselmänner*; the term is too embedded in shame to be used by someone who testifies. She comments that

> one needs a moral distinction between the drowned and the saved, a "we" and a "they," to hide the guilt and shame of having survived one's own death. This distinction is manifest precisely at the level of testimony, when the body translates into the corpus of writing. It is in this sense, the ethical one, that the survivors perceive their testimony as incomplete. The lacuna in survivor narratives is testimony from *inside* the experience of the *Muselmann*.[27]

It is precisely the tension between the "we" and the "they" that Levi explores in his representation of the *Muselmänner*, and the lack of a testimonial subject is underscored in his portrait of the *Muselmänner*. In *Survival in Auschwitz*, Levi does not initially use the term, but instead introduces us to the concept through a fellow prisoner who, tellingly, is known not by his name but only through part of his number. Levi begins the chapter in which this prisoner is introduced, "Ka-Be" (Infirmary), with a curious reversal, as he describes the masters and slaves working all around him in the infernal system of the camp, and ends the opening paragraphs by declaring that "all are our enemies or our rivals." There is a blank space of separation on the page, then Levi begins again by negating this very statement: "No, I honestly don't feel that my companion of today, yoked with me under the same load, is either enemy or rival."[28] Yet he continues with a reductive and pejorative description of his companion Null Achtzehn, Zero Eighteen: "as if everyone were aware that only a man is worthy of a name, and that Null Achtzehn is no longer a man. I think that even he has forgotten his name – certainly he acts as if this were so."[29]

In his initial introduction to Null Achtzehn, Levi has doubly marginalized him from the outset: stating that he is not worthy of a name, and then presuming that he does not remember his name, thus projecting the results of being known by a number instead of a name. Levi continues:

> He is indifferent to the point where he doesn't trouble to avoid labor or blows or to search for food. He carries out every order he is given, and it's

predictable that when they send him to his death he will go with the same total indifference.[30]

Levi's description of Null Achtzehn furnishes the preface to the story of how Levi became injured due to the other's clumsiness, as Levi recounts how the other tripped and caused Levi's foot to be mangled by the heavy steel piling they were carrying together. This foot injury leads directly into the episode of Levi's time in Ka-Be, the infirmary. Before introducing us to this prisoner without a name, Levi has explained the importance of choosing the right work partner. The consequences of the wrong work partner are made obvious in this episode, as it has resulted in his trip to the infirmary.

These consequences, however, go beyond bodily difficulties. As their partnership proves to be physically dangerous for Levi, so does the very presence of a *Muselmann* before him prove dangerous in other ways. The antagonism embedded in Levi's statements and presumptions about Null Achtzehn serves as a distancing manoeuvre. Levi effectively sets up two categories: prisoners like him who are proactive in the search for survival, and those who are not. The latter are not to be pitied or understood: compassion is withheld and scorn, hostility, and the dehumanization of name deprivation are found in its place. To state at the outset that Null Achtzehn is neither enemy nor rival, in effect to put him in a kind of limbo, seems disingenuous given the foot injury Levi suffers. It appears that he does in fact serve the function of an enemy, albeit unwittingly.

The more insidious consequences of Levi's exposure to a *Muselmann* are made clear only later in the text, in the chapter entitled "The Drowned and the Saved." Levi brings up Null Achtzehn's name again, this time in the context of his more general discussion of the *Muselmänner*: "If some Null Achtzehn totters, he will find no one to extend a hand; on the contrary, someone will knock him aside, because it is in no one's interest that there be one more *Muselmann* dragging himself to work every day."[31] From this overtly hostile position towards Null Achtzehn, Levi continues by describing the *Muselmänner* as

non-men who march and labor in silence, the divine spark dead within them, already too empty to truly suffer. One hesitates to call them living; one hesitates to call their death death – in the face of it they have no fear, because they are too tired to understand. They crowd my memory with their faceless presence.[32]

He continues by visualizing them as symbolic of the dehumanization done to humankind:

> If I could encompass all the evil of our time in one image, I would choose this image, which is familiar to me: an emaciated man, head bowed and shoulders bent, on whose face and in whose eyes no trace of thought can be seen.[33]

At first reading, Levi's eloquent description of what has happened to the *Muselmänner* seems to be consonant with his usually humanitarian and compassionate understanding of the damage done to humankind in the camp. But further consideration reveals a concern in the identification of the *Muselmänner* with ultimate evil. This group is represented as carrying the physical stigmata of evil, showing the worst that the Nazi system could do to still living human beings. Yet were they responsible for their condition? Levi appears to suggest that perhaps they were responsible, and casts them into a position uncomfortably close to that of a scapegoat. From one side, they are disliked by prisoners, who are afraid of ending up like them and blame them for a lack of energy that could potentially improve their condition; from the other side they are viewed as embodying the evil of the camp. The reasons for their lack of initiative are clearly beyond their control, but nonetheless they are made to pay a price for this. They are physically branded with the stigma of what has been done to them.

Along with many other survivor/writers, Levi appears to have little empathy for this type of victim. He uses the image of the *Muselmann*, bowed down, without thought, as the image of evil in our day. This perhaps suggests a confusion of the "outside," the camp system, with the "inside," or the victim of the system. The victim is desubjectified a second time through Levi's portrayal. The *Muselmann* is the result of what evil has wrought, not evil itself, yet this description suggests otherwise. Is Levi mistaking affect for identity? Can the two be in fact separated? There is an active rejection of the identity of the *Muselmänner*, even though he tells us that it is the identity of most of the camp inmates. They are without a face in his representation of them, as he says, "they crowd my memory with their faceless presence." But we must consider precisely who and what actually makes them faceless. Levi's narrative strategy ultimately removes their subjectivity.

The *Muselmänner* literally embody shame, both in the sense of utter dehumanization and in the way they are represented as both shamed and shaming. The specularity of their shame thus reflects both on their own responsibility for their condition and on the outside forces that made them this way. There is also a potential contradiction in Levi's description: if the *Muselmann's* head is bowed, how can the others see that there is no trace of thought on his face?

Consonni has written on the centrality of the bodily testimony of the *Muselmänner* in the lager experience, in a manner essential to the question of linguistic testimony as well, commenting, "challenging the notion of the witness as a speaker, a narrator, I treat the *Muselmann* as an integral witness."[34] In her reading, the physical body itself testifies. She also affirms the following:

> In the transition from the body of the *Muselmann* to the *corpus* of writing the *Muselmann's* body is transcended, even at the price of a lacuna in the texture of memory. The resistance of the survivors to remembering themselves as bodies being-towards-death suggests their avoidance of full engagement with their experience. It is safer for them to represent the *Muselmann* as the ultimate "other," a body unknown to them, an eternal stranger.[35]

The *Muselmänner* are thus held at a distance because of their seeming indifference towards death and their lack of initiative in trying to save themselves. They also bear the frightening bodily marks of their condition.

Joseph Farrell has pointed out the differences between Levi's statements regarding this category of prisoner and victim in his earlier work in contrast to his later essay, "Shame," affirming that Levi's more mature reflections on the *Muselmänner* are harsher than his earlier portrayals.[36] What also need to be taken into consideration, however, are the contradictions and reversals found within Levi's discourse of the *Muselmänner*, even within his earlier text. As Consonni notes:

> Primo Levi comes close to talking about himself as a *Muselmann* in the last chapter of *If This Is a Man*, in an account of the camp just abandoned by the SS in retreat. Here his *Muselmanns* are first referred to by the excluding third-person "they": "ragged, decrepit, skeleton-like patients at all able to move dragged themselves everywhere on the frozen soil, like an invasion of worms ... no longer in control of their own bowels, they had fouled everywhere, polluting the precious snow" ... Soon afterwards however, the *Muselmanns* are referred to in the inclusive first-person plural: "Other

starving spectres like ourselves wandered around searching, unshaven, with hollow eyes, grey skeletons, bones in rags."[37]

As further evidence of Levi's deep ambivalence towards this figure, Antony Rowland points out that Levi himself is actually described as a *Muselmann* in two instances in *Survival in Auschwitz*: first by the nurse at Ka-Be and then by Alex after his chemistry examination.[38]

What has turned into a de facto companion text to Levi's already difficult statements on shame is a text of even more problematic statements on the subject, Agamben's *Remnants of Auschwitz*. Agamben's text has had such a pervasive influence that it is now difficult to consider one without the other. Critical reactions to Agamben have been strong, ranging from adoringly hagiographic to outraged.[39] I would also argue that Agamben's text has become a cipher for reactions to Levi that critics have not felt comfortable expressing. Agamben addresses the question of shame in Levi's thought, productively at times, but in a manner that ultimately and problematically conflates the witness, the reader, and the figure of the *Muselmann*.

In one particularly egregious misreading of Levi, Agamben claims that in Levi's gray zone, the victims and the perpetrators are the same. Yet Levi makes it clear that he does not hold the two groups to the same standard, and that we must suspend judgment of those who engaged in collaboration in order to survive. As Leys puts it, "Levi opposes the conflation between the roles of executioner and victim on which Agamben appears to insist … there is thus a considerable distance between Agamben's view of the gray zone as a zone of irresponsibility where all the traditional categories of ethics no longer apply and victim and perpetrator form a single homogenous group, and Levi's more nuanced position."[40] Thomas Trezise argues that Agamben fails – or refuses – to recognize the structure of Levi's gray zone as determined by the camp hierarchy.[41] Levi's position is in fact diametrically opposed to that which Agamben claims for him, as Stefano Levi Della Torre asserts in his essay on Agamben's text.[42]

Despite this puzzling and outrageous misreading of Levi, there is a useful element to Agamben's assessment of the ethical position of the *Muselmänner*, as he considers what he calls the "paradoxical ethical situation":

to deny the *Muselmänner* humanity would be to accept the verdict of the SS and to repeat their gesture. The *Muselmann* has, instead, moved into a zone of the human where not only help but also dignity and self-respect have become useless. But if there is a zone of the human in which these concepts make no sense, then they are not genuine ethical concepts, for no ethics can claim to exclude a part of humanity, no matter how unpleasant or difficult that humanity is to see.[43]

Levi's ethics do in fact appear to exclude the *Muselmänner* from consideration. Seen as emblematic of the destructive powers of the camp, they are viewed not as individuals but as a dehumanized mass. Levi's description of them as "faceless" emphasizes their presumed state of being already dead, incapable of thought. The way in which he represents them raises the question of whether he separates a critique of the system from a critique of the victim.

Let's look for a moment at alternatives to becoming a *Muselmann*, as Levi describes them. What are the options for the prisoners? Levi gives us some contradictory messages regarding this. In the chapter "The Drowned and the Saved," he tells us that if you don't somehow acquire privilege, you become a *Muselmann*: "Anyone who does not know how to become an Organisator, Kombinator, Prominent (the eloquence of these words!) soon becomes a Muselmann."[44] Those who become prominent are, however, implicated in a moral gray zone that he describes with great detail, both in this chapter and in his later essay of the same name. Paradoxically, the same initiative that can prevent the prisoner from becoming a *Muselmann* is what can take him from the realm of the entirely innocent to the realm of the morally ambiguous.

Our understanding of Levi's writings on the *Muselmänner* is informed by our own subject position as readers engaged in what has been described as secondary witnessing through these images, horrified by the destruction and inhumanity of the Holocaust.[45] As stated above, the *Musselmänner* are made to represent the excess of evil done to the victims in the camps. They are doubly horrific because, as Levi presents them, they are the walking dead, the "divine spark" already extinguished: a concept harder to bear than the actual dead, as Agamben points out. Furthermore, Levi states that they do not even merit memory: "they die or disappear, leaving no trace in anyone's memory."[46] But if we reject this sweeping representation of mass evil and begin to consider these prisoners as individuals, we might well wonder how it is that Levi and other testimonial writers can assert with such certitude that these prisoners are beyond thought and are already dead.

There are two important questions that arise upon consideration of the "already dead" *Muselmänner*. The first is the issue of what it means to speak for the *Muselmänner* in this way: what, for example, is the effect upon our concept of their subjectivity? They have been reduced twice: once by the dehumanizing camp system, and the second time through testimony that insists upon a repetition and even a furthering of this same dehumanization. The camp system sought to dehumanize them, and the testimony concretizes this effort through describing them as already dead.

The second question is, what happens if the *Muselmänner* actually survive their state? Like some figures such as the child Hurbinek, for whom Levi openly acknowledges that his words serve as his memory, the *Muselmänner* are portrayed as a done deal, already dead from all significant points of view, and a death that is itself diminished, as Levi goes so far as to say "one hesitates to call their death death."[47] What distinguishes the human from the bestial has apparently been extinguished. But what happens if they come back? What does "already dead" actually mean? Can a *Muselmann* be resuscitated from the "living dead"?

Agamben provides an appendix to *Remnants of Auschwitz* containing ten testimonies from alleged former *Muselmänner*. When one reads these testimonies, two points at once become obvious. The first is that the very criteria that distinguish the *Muselmänner* from other prisoners become quite indistinct. The testimonies range from those who, like Levi, struggled for their survival by looking for extra food and taking care of themselves as best they were able, to those who became apathetic and appeared sense-dead from the outside. Clearly, however, the writers of these testimonies were nonetheless able to survive.

The first "*Muselmann*" quoted, Lucjan Sobieraj, defines the state through his single-minded search for food:

> I can't forget the days when I was a *Muselmann*. I was weak, exhausted, dead tired. I saw something to eat wherever I looked … The head of the barracks and the other inmates who had positions threw out their potato skins, sometimes even a whole potato. I used to watch them secretly and look for the skins in the trash so that I could eat them. I would spread jam on them; they were really good.[48]

It seems clear that planning to obtain, searching for, and successfully finding extra food are the acts of someone trying to survive, not of a "walking dead" person incapable of thought and thus, one would presume, of strategizing survival in the way in which this prisoner did ("I used to watch them secretly"). How does this statement differ from the testimony of a "successful" prisoner, one who did not consider himself a *Muselmann*, and how does this testimony change our understanding of what a *Muselmann* is? According to this testimony, the category of *Muselmann* appears to some degree to be self-elected and self-defined as well as imposed from the outside. This notion, however, goes against everything that both Agamben and Levi are saying about the *Muselmann*. Another former *Muselmann* affirms that he would stretch into certain positions to try to avoid pneumonia, once again actively participating in a survival strategy.[49]

A longer testimony by Bronislaw Goscinki discusses the definition of the *Muselmänner* and what set them apart from other prisoners. They were chiefly concerned with getting food and not much else, he states; they were not interested in speaking of life outside the camp, but rather were focused on day-to-day survival.[50] Only about half of the testimonies reported by Agamben conform to Levi's definition of a *Muselmann*, someone who has become so apathetic and disinterested that they do not attempt to improve their state by acquiring extra food or making the work lighter. The rest of the testimonies in the appendix recount the everyday struggle for survival in which human faculties are fully engaged.[51] This has the curious effect of undoing Agamben's conclusions about Levi's paradox right at the end of Agamben's text: these testimonies serve as a cogent arguments against the very theory Agamben is proposing. They speak as well to the practical and ethical impossibility of Levi's definition of the *Muselmänner* as "nonhuman."

The second point that becomes obvious on reading Agamben's appendix has to do with Levi and Agamben's definition of the *Muselmann* as a creature incapable of thought. If the *Muselmänner* are by definition beings deprived of thought, how can they later testify to a condition in which human qualities do not exist? If thought does not exist within the condition of the *Muselmann*, can it be said that memory of that time can exist? Yet it is apparently possible for a *Muselmann* to survive and then bear testimony to a condition said to be beyond thought or even life. That this survival is an exception rather than the rule is clear, but through these testimonies the appendix nonetheless furnishes voices of the presumed, but rather lively, dead. This is a paradox that far outreaches the one presented by Levi and analysed by Agamben: that the *Muselmänner* are the only true witnesses, yet cannot testify.

Jeffrey Mehlman affirms the following:

Now there is a central paradox, according to Agamben ... on the one hand, [the *Muselmann*] is the person who has experienced the camp at its worst – and is thus the "complete witness." On the other, his state of near autistic degradation ... made him the least trustworthy of speakers. He is essentially speechless. But if such be the case, then the only witness is disqualified, through a kind of epistemological hitch, on logical grounds. In Agamben's words, "Let us, indeed posit Auschwitz, that to which it is not possible to bear witness; and let us also posit the Muselmann as the absolute impossibility of bearing witness" ... Has a memorialist of the genocide ever come closer to the position of a Holocaust denier?[52]

Mehlman also discusses Agamben's refusal to engage the testimony left by the *Sonderkommando*, the *Meguiles Auschwitz*, which refers to the testimony they left buried at Auschwitz. Even though the ranks of the *Sonderkommando* were purged periodically, some of them did succeed in leaving behind their testimony.[53] How then can they not be considered full witnesses to the crime of genocide? Agamben writes that "the untestifiable, that to which no one has borne witness, has a name. In the jargon of the camp, it is *der Muselmann*."[54] It's hard to fathom why Agamben chooses to focus solely on the *Muselmann* as the only true witness, and why he chooses to twist Levi's thought to fit his own theory.[55]

Manuela Consonni puts the matter somewhat differently, through the following categorization of the *Muselmann*:

Dori Laub wrote that the process of witnessing involves three different yet possibly simultaneous stages: "the level of being a witness to oneself within the experience, the level of being a witness to the testimonies of others, and the level of being a witness to the process of witnessing itself" ... The survivor is, indeed, three in one: a flesh-witness, an eye-witness, and a witness of witnessing.[56]

Consonni's analysis is particularly useful in that it recoups the *Muselmann* as a speaking subject, albeit through a bodily representation, which directly argues against the kind of desubjectification expressed in survivor testimonies and in Agamben's work.

This new paradox brings us to a point of crisis not easily resolved, and highlights the problem of uncritical readings of survivor testimony that leave aside issues such as what appears to be a highly prejudicial representation of the *Muselmann*. I will propose a new model of looking at their representation that may be useful.

In the British and American legal system, the concept of the adverse witness is juridical. An adverse or hostile witness is one who pretends not to remember, or is reluctant or afraid to testify, and so the rules for questioning this type of witness change in order to better allow the lawyers to tease out the truth. Once declared an adverse witness, the person can be asked direct questions by the prosecutor, a process normally forbidden in court when the witness is cooperating and his or her testimony is therefore favourable to either the defence or prosecution. Direct questions, often described as leading questions, are those that presume a certain narrative and that are designed to confirm it, for example, "Did you see the man in the gray coat speaking to the victim around 8 p.m. on the evening in question?" as opposed to a more general invitation to recount a narrative: "What did you see at 8 p.m. that evening?"

Reflecting on the notion of the adverse witness as a discursive model is useful in understanding Levi's attitude towards the *Muselmänner*. If we think of the survivors who write about the *Muselmänner* as adverse to them, it changes the questions we may feel comfortable asking of the text of testimony. Before considering this category, our implied interrogation of the text as readers might sound like this: Can you tell the world what was different about the *Muselmänner*? What were the effects of dehumanization on them?

Direct questions, however, could sound like the following: Why do you describe the *Muselmänner* as already dead? Why do you assume that Null Achtzehn was unworthy of a name or of thought? How can you reasonably project a lack of thought onto another person? When questions like these are posed, a deeper answer may be forthcoming about the motivations that underlie the ways in which the *Muselmänner* are represented. The principal motivation behind the hostile attitude towards the *Muselmänner* is perhaps obvious: fear and a taboo reaction, discussed very briefly in Agamben, but whose consequences are not fully teased out in that text and not mentioned at all in Levi's work. As Joseph Farrell has remarked:

> Whatever the *Muselmann* in Auschwitz finally represents, the most disconcerting element – for the contemporary reader – in the written records is a distancing which borders on, and frequently becomes

synonymous with, contempt. Gitta Sereny, in her interview with Franz Stangl, commandant of Treblinka, found that people like him had entertained the same feelings.[57]

Agamben comments, "According to the law that what man despises is also what he fears resembles him, the M is universally avoided because everyone in the camp recognizes himself in his disfigured face."[58] The *Muselmann* appears to be a figure that attracts and repels at the same time. Levi is drawn towards it as the figure of nihilism, perhaps as a respite from the moral strain of witnessing. He metaphorically kills the figure who is the only true witness in order to make this possible, describing the *Muselmann* as already dead. The counterargument is that Levi, and other writers, are appalled by what the Nazis have done to the *Muselmänner* so that the description of them as already dead is a way of witnessing crimes against them, a way of recounting atrocity. The question of the *Muselmänner*'s individual dignity and subjectivity, however, goes unanswered by this approach.

In *Survival in Auschwitz*, soon after his arrival Levi has a meaningful encounter with a sergeant named Steinlauf. The older man teaches him the importance of maintaining at least the appearance of hygiene by washing even if there is no soap or towels, as this effort fights directly against the dehumanization of the camp. As Levi comments after he has been imparted this wisdom, "we still possess one power, and we must defend it with all our strength, for it is the last – the power to refuse our consent."[59] It is perhaps what Levi sees as the *voluntary* giving of consent to the dehumanization and eventual massacre that he finds most offensive in the *Muselmänner*.

What is at stake in the representation of the *Muselmänner*? Berel Lang remarks that "the moral strain within the literary project, and between it and the historical subject, will disclose itself in the process of representation."[60] He also looks at "writing itself as an occasion of moral judgement. Once writing is viewed as an act, to be judged for what it 'does' to its subject and to its readers, then the enormity of the Nazi genocide in its historical character or nonliterary character necessarily affects – enlarges – the risks incurred in its literary representation."[61] The perils inherent in literary representation of the Holocaust thus cut two ways: both what is represented and how it is represented run the risks that Lang describes. This is particularly clear in Levi's representation of the *Muselmänner*, in particular when we consider his use of the trope of the Medusa in conjunction with the *Muselmänner*.

The Medusa and the *Muselmänner*

As is so common in Levi's work, when the text shows great strain, he refers to classical literature and mythology as an epistemological model, even, at times, to refute it.[62] Levi uses the image of the Gorgon, the Medusa, to speak of those who perished or who returned unable to tell the story, in direct contrast to witnesses who are able to recount what happened. As a figure of paradox, as well as one of representation, the appearance of Medusa takes on crucial proportions in the passages in which Levi discusses the *Muselmänner* and the *Sonderkommando* and their ability to testify.

In "The Gray Zone," Levi says the following about the surviving *Sonderkommando*, using the figure of the Medusa, as he discusses their narrative capabilities:

> From men who have known this extreme destitution one cannot expect a deposition in the legal sense of the term but, rather, something between a complaint, a curse, atonement, and the impulse to justify, to rehabilitate oneself. What should be expected is a liberating outburst rather than truth with the face of Medusa.[63]

In this passage he conflates the face of Medusa with the message coming from those who have not survived: the truth would be spoken by the victims, yet it is the face of Medusa that stands for them, that speaks a paralysing truth. Levi speaks directly against survivors' testifying in a "legal sense," presumably thus meaning a factual one, because to do so would be devastating and they could not "rehabilitate" themselves. This is a truly intriguing passage, as it gives the reader insight into Levi's perception of the relationship between extreme trauma, the telling of the story, and the changed identity of the survivor. The person who has experienced trauma as severe as that of the *Sonderkommando*, those who ran the crematoria and often encountered their murdered loved ones in the process, cannot tell the story without resorting to atonement, lamenting, and cursing because they must recover their lost selves. The story must thus adjust to the needs of the survivor who tells it: it must be liberating in order to achieve the rehabilitation, the regaining of that lost self. The story is not driven by a testimonial and historical impulse that stands outside individual need: it is rather the need that shapes the story. How can we read this statement in conjunction with the way in which he uses the trope of the Gorgon in "Shame"?

Here the "face of Medusa" is that which tells the terrible truth, not that which represents evil. This second invocation of the figure of Medusa is found in the already quoted passage from "Shame":

> Let me repeat that we, the survivors, are not the true witnesses. This is a troublesome notion that I became aware of gradually by reading other people's memoirs and rereading my own years later. We survivors are an anomalous and negligible minority. We are the ones who, because of our transgressions, ability, or luck, did not touch bottom. The ones who did, who saw the Gorgon, did not come back to tell, or they came back mute. But it is they, the "Muselmänner," the drowned, the witnesses to everything – they are the ones whose testimony would have had a comprehensive meaning. They are the rule, we are the exception.[64]

Levi's point of reference for the Medusa, given his affinity for the medieval poet, is quite likely canto 9 of Dante's *Inferno*. He first references this passage by mentioning the Furies in his chapter on memory, in relation to injuries that cannot be healed, that constitute a permanent trauma for the survivor, evoking "the Furies, in whom we are forced to believe."[65] In Dante's text, the Furies appear and see Dante and Virgil approaching, as they come to the gates of lower Hell. The Furies, figures that are half woman, half serpent, call upon Medusa to dispatch Dante and Virgil. Virgil first admonishes Dante to cover his eyes, and then adds his own hands over Dante's eyes to be sure that his vision is entirely blocked:

"Vegna Medusa: sì 'l farem di smalto,"
dicevan tutte riguardando in giuso;
"mal non vengiammo in Teseo l'assalto."

"Volgiti 'n dietro e tien lo viso chiuso;
ché se 'l Gorgón si mostra e tu 'l vedessi,
nulla sarebbe di tornar mai suso."

Così disse 'l maestro; ed elli stessi
mi volse, e non si tenne a le mie mani,
che con le sue ancor non mi chiudessi.

O voi ch'avete li 'ntelletti sani,
mirate la dottrina che s'asconde
sotto 'l velame de li versi strani.

"Let Medusa come
and we'll turn him
to stone," they cried, looking
down. "To our cost,
we failed to avenge
the assault of Theseus."
"Turn your back and
keep your eyes
shut,
for if the Gorgon
head appears and
should you see it,
all chance for your
return above is
lost."
While my master
spoke he turned me
round
and, placing no trust
in my own hands,
covered my face with
his hands also.
O you who have
sound intellects, consider the teaching
that is hidden
behind the veil of
these strange verses.[66]

Virgil covers Dante's eyes so that he doesn't see the Medusa, "if the Gorgon head appears." The threat of the Medusa in the canto is about what you can see and what you cannot permit yourself to see: proper vision that can lead to purification, or the wrong vision that leads to petrification. The Medusa is thus a figure that represents what is most frightening to Dante: loss of perspective, loss of vision, loss of life.

The passage that follows, regarding the "hidden" teaching, has engendered much discussion among Dante critics. Does it refer to the entire poem, to the episodes preceding this moment, or it is a call to the future? John Freccero looks at the meaning of the hidden *dottrina* as related specifically to the entire poem. He associates the Medusa, or rather her evocation because she does not in fact appear, with the following interpretation:

> The temporality we sense in the threat of the Medusa is a representation of the threat of the temporality of retrospection, of a danger narrowly averted ... such a temporality is the essence of the descent into hell, the past seen under the aspect of death. The traditional threat on all such journeys is the threat of nostalgia ... Moreover, the threat is not merely a petrification, but also a *no return*: "Nulla sarebbe del tornar mai suso."[67]

If the Medusa is hiding a secret teaching for Levi, what would it be? His adoption of the figures of the Furies and the Medusa puts forward that they represent the teaching of the meaning of death in the camps. Levi uses the Furies to indicate that the loss, the injury to the survivor inflicted by the Shoah is permanent, while he simultaneously affirms the paralysing effect of evil upon the *Muselmänner*, those who have touched bottom, and the survivor who lives to write about it. Freccero's interpretation of the Medusa as embodying the threat of the temporal nature of retrospection is also useful here, especially in relation to Levi's discussion of the *Sonderkommando* and their need to recoup their damaged selves. Retrospection for them, and often for other survivors as well, is a luxury best avoided.

In Dante's text the Medusa never appears; the mere mention of her is enough to cause Virgil to shield Dante's eyes. But in Levi's imaginative rewriting, in his concentrationary world, the Medusa does appear, and more than once. She is not just a threat: in Levi's imaginative lexicon, she is quite real.

Why does Levi find the Medusa to be such a compelling figure? And even more to the point, why the pairing of the *Muselmänner* and the Medusa? Often referred to by the more generic name of the Gorgon, from the Greek for "dreadful," Medusa appears in texts ranging from Dante to Shakespeare, to Freud to Derrida. Examining what they call her "persistent fascination" in their volume of responses to the Medusa, Nancy Vickers and Marjorie Garber point out the contradictory and often enigmatic ways in which writers have for centuries been fascinated by her story:

> Poets have called her a Muse. Feminists have adopted her as sign of powerful womanhood. Anthropologists read her image as embedded in the paradoxical logic of amulets, talismans, and relics. Psychoanalysts

have understood the serpents wreathing her head as a symbol of the fear of castration ... The most canonical writers (Homer, Dante, Shakespeare, Goethe, Shelley) have invoked her story and sung both her praise and her blame.[68]

One of three Gorgons and famed for her beauty, in particular her gorgeous locks of hair, Medusa succumbs to the blandishments of Zeus (or Jupiter, depending on the version of the story) within the temple of Minerva (or Athena), thereby defiling the temple. To punish her for this transgression, as a gesture of shaming her, Athena turns her hair into serpents and gives her the power to turn anyone who looks at her into stone by virtue of the horror of those snakes. It should not go without saying that the god who seduced her seems not to have suffered any punishment himself.[69]

The problem of the defilement of the temple is turned into a much larger problem: no one can dispatch the now enraged and horrified Medusa, because to look at her means certain death. After many stoic attempts are made, all doomed to failure, Athena, who is obviously the mastermind of the scheme, gives Perseus the bright idea of using her reflection to locate her and then decapitate her. The representation of Medusa found on his shining shield has no power to petrify, and Perseus cuts off her head, bearing it proudly aloft on his shield. Yet the head retains its ability to petrify even after the death of the subject, which raises the issue of what death actually means *to* and *for* the Medusa, and how her representation ultimately functions.

Medusa works as a figure of representation and its dangers from several points of view, beginning with her death at the hands of Perseus. Medusa *as her own agent* has been killed; in other words, she no longer controls who receives her gaze, she has lost her subjectivity, similar to the *Muselmänner*. Becoming an object and a tool, to wit *the* Medusa, her head continues to be used by Perseus as a weapon against his own enemies.

Questions pertinent to representation and also to testimony are overwhelmingly present in Medusa's story. What is particularly compelling is the notion that the reflection of the live Medusa in the shield is not dangerous, yet physical re-creations of the dead Medusa retain the original power of the head. In her analysis of the power of the Medusa legend, Camille Dumoulié writes:

Medusa's head, an apparently simple motif linked to the myth of Perseus, was freed through being severed and cut loose from its "moorings" by the hero in the remote depths of the world. There is something paradoxical about the story since the monster was all the more indestructible because it had been killed. Indeed, the figure of Medusa is characterized by paradox, both in terms of the actual mythical stare, which turned men to stone, and in the interpretations that have been given to it. The fascination that she exerts arises from a combination of beauty and horror. Her head was used, in ancient times, as an apotropaic mask – a sort of talisman which both killed and redeemed.[70]

The concept of the apotropaic, that which protects against evil, is a central part of the Medusa legend. The Medusa can thus be understood as presenting a compelling relation to Shoah testimony, borne out by Levi's use of her in his text. According to Levi, her gaze of evil turns the *Muselmänner* to stone, and thus unable to testify. This same gaze, however, also functions as a trope for the representability of the Shoah that is, itself, apotropaic. How the Medusa functions as a figure for Shoah testimony provides an original and compelling reading of Levi's stance on the *Muselmänner* as those victims who cannot testify, alive or dead.

Shoah testimony is often viewed as invested with the power to ward off evil through issuing warnings regarding the potential of repeating a history that has devastated not only millions of lives, but the meaning of civility itself. Testimony is often defined as healing for the author as well as instructive for the reader, a stance that Levi fully embraces in his writings, and so it bears a heavy weight of expectation in terms of its ability to heal the rupture of trauma.

The two-sided nature of the Gorgon reflects a basic paradox of testimony: what cannot be represented has to be represented. As Leigh Gilmore states:

> Survivors of trauma are urged to testify repeatedly to their trauma in an effort to create the language that will manifest and contain trauma as well as the witnesses who will recognize it … Language is asserted as that which can realize trauma even as it is theorized as that which fails in the face of trauma … For the survivor of trauma such an ambivalence can amount to an impossible injunction to tell what cannot, in this view, be spoken.[71]

The gaze of the Gorgon and the gaze of testimony both involve a high level of risk for the viewer. Dumoulie asserts, "the Gorgon also represents what cannot be represented, i.e. death, which it is impossible to see or to look at … guarding the doorway to the world of the dead, she prevents the living from entering."[72] Levi establishes the Gorgon as that which either literally or metaphorically kills the voice of witness, by rendering that voice mute. Interestingly, Levi appears to place both of these conditions – perished or silent – on the same level. Both are, for the purposes of testimony, equally devastating. And here there is an even stronger connection between the Gorgon and the status of testimony: the Gorgon represents death, precisely that condition which makes testimony impossible but also is at the heart of the paradox Levi sets up. In his textual logic, the *Muselmänner* are the true witnesses because they have died at the hands of the Nazis, which then makes their testimony impossible.

There are three main paradoxes at the heart of the trope that Levi uses to describe the impossibility and the risk of testimony. The first is the Medusa herself, who protects and kills at the same time, and her very origin betrays another paradox, that of her representation in a shield, an image that is visible but not tangible. In other words, that representation has no power for her – quite the opposite, as it empowers her killer. She can thus be done in through her own representation.

The second is the paradox of Shoah literature. Those texts must inform and protect through that informing, yet its representation is never up to its own task: trauma cannot find a language that can represent, yet it must represent all the same.

The third paradox is the one that Levi openly sets forth in his essay: the true witnesses are all gone, victims of the Gorgon, the evil, and so they cannot testify, yet testimony is present in Levi's own words. Those who saw the Gorgon either did not survive, or could not testify – and Levi comes very close to suggesting that those two outcomes are the same, that the fate of returning mute is equivalent to not returning at all. The testimonial identity is thus fully invested with the mandate of telling the story, a mandate that is posited as equally important to survival itself.

There is one more important connection to be made between Levi's construct of the limits of testimony and the figure he uses to explore that limit, which is the notion of shame that is embedded in the Medusa story. Medusa's shame at the hands of Athena is a double-edged sword: she has lost her famed beauty, but the price – or benefit? – of that is the power to kill whoever looks at her. This can be read as shame's ultimate revenge: rather than bowing her head in shame over her now utterly destroyed beauty, she kills with a glance that is the opposite of the posture of shame. Her functioning as a meta-phor for the evil of the camp thus literally embodies the question of shame. The lost shame of the *Muselmänner* – because part of the issue here is that they apparently have no shame over their dehumanized condition – is transferred onto this executionary figure who embodies the very opposite of shame.

In both instances, the Medusa is adopted as the figure of a truth so terrible that the witness to it cannot survive. The high risk of the testi-monial enterprise is underscored by Levi's use of the Gorgon as a figure for what cannot be recounted, as testimony is necessary, apotropaic, and risky. These risks in a small way may also be seen as extending to the reader. What is at stake for the survivor who does testify, and also for the reader confronted with the *Muselmänner*, is made explicit by Consonni in a discussion of survivors' apparent discomfort with the *Muselmänner* and their desire to distance themselves from them:

> This is also safer for us as readers. Our inability, or unwillingness, to imagine the bodily being-towards-death is an extension of the survivors' experience and not only a matter of linguistic predicament.[73]

The witness to atrocity is shamed on several counts. He/she has seen the shame of the reduction of the *Muselmänner*: shamed because he could have been there in the sense of participating in the same fate, and shamed because he *was* there physically, and saw the presumed shame of the other. From this point of view, the witness is implicated in the shame of the *Muselmann* by his refusal to identify with this figure and, at the same time, implicated in the shame by the paralysing impossibil-ity of not identifying. This juxtapositioning highlights as well the moral ground of shame, as Henry Knight puts it: "The recognition of shame, as shame, is an experience of the moral claim of the other on the one experiencing the shame."[74] We might well call this specular shame: the effect on the one witnessing that shame.

Levi ends his essay on shame with these words:

> There is another, greater shame, the shame of the world ... there are those who turn their backs on their own transgressions and those of others, to avoid seeing or being touched by them. This is how most Germans behaved in the twelve years of Hitler, in the illusion that not seeing was not knowing, and that not knowing relieved them of their own share of complicity or connivance.[75]

Levi contrasts the shame of the people who stood by or actively collaborated with the state of the survivors, who are "denied the shield of willful ignorance."[76] The survivors have no choice but to know: and Levi strongly implies that shame is the consequence of knowing. And not only for the survivor.

In the end, Levi conflates the figure of the Medusa with the figure of the *Muselmann*. Both are desubjectified; both can paralyse through their very presence, and both embody the evil of the camps. But his use of the Medusa in the case of the *Sonderkommando* differs from that in the case of the *Muselmann*. The distance between the two is just different enough to bring to mind a distinction that Levi explores in a very different text:

> You must not trust the almost-the-same ..., the practically the same, the nearly, the or, any surrogates or stopgaps. The differences may be small but can lead to radically diverse results, like railroad switches.[77]

As a theory of writing and of representation, Levi's own words about small differences is revealing in this particular context: here, his use of the trope of the Medusa is just dissimilar enough to say very different things about the two groups he uses it to represent. For the *Sonderkommando*, were they able to testify factually, they would become the mouthpiece of the Medusa, they would speak its terrible and paralysing truth. On the one hand, for the *Sonderkommando* the Medusa is the figure of evil that their testimony would become; on the other hand, the Medusa is the figure for the effects of evil for the decrepit and mute or deceased *Muselmänner*.

This constitutes a fine distinction; yet what appears to be almost the same, namely his use of the Medusa in one passage and the Gorgon in the other, speaks volumes about his very different assessments of these two groups. Dumoulié's comment regarding the status of the Medusa after her death, "the monster was all the more indestructible because it had been killed," could refer to the representational fate of the *Muselmänner* as well. Feared, held in contempt, held to be already dead before their time but whose death is not death, not even held as a trace in anyone's memory when they are gone, they are swept away as an anonymous mass. The *Muselmänner*, like the Medusa made horrific in her innocence and then used to evil ends, are victimized a second time through these representations and bear no little resemblance to the trope Levi uses to explore what has been done to them. They are unable to testify, thus conveying the end of "true" testimony as he articulates it. The *Sonderkommando*, on the other hand, would *become* the Medusa if they *could* give a factual testimony: "What should be expected is a liberating outburst rather than truth with the face of Medusa." They become the face of Medusa, their testimony would paralyse if it could be recounted. One group cannot testify because they returned mute or did not return at all, the other cannot testify because that knowledge would paralyse the listener and make a return to the living impossible for the survivor.

The Medusa represents not only the evil of the camp, the impossibility of returning if one has seen the bottom where the Gorgon resides, but also the threat of the knowledge of the evil. That knowledge is paralysing, and ultimately impossible to absorb if the self of the survivor who has seen it is ever to be regained. The exigencies of testimony and the impossibility of a selfless autobiography are thus bound up with the figuration of a shame that speaks simultaneously to the need for testimony and the need for silence. Viewed through the lens of the Medusa that Levi give us, the task of testimony is highly vexed and bound up with the impossibility of an autobiography that could truly speak for and to a divided self.

Chapter Six

Conclusion:
Cautionary Tales: Early Poetry

As a conclusion to this study of Primo Levi's identities as a survivor and as a writer, I'm going to return to the beginning of his opus: two very early poems he wrote about his Auschwitz experiences. The first, "Buna," engages the themes that will remain at the heart of his opus.[1] In particular, it postulates that the gaze of the survivor towards his lost companions is a treacherous one and invites peril. "Buna" was finished on 28 December 1945, a date that appears at the end of the poem. It was subsequently published on 22 June 1946 in the regional newspaper *L'amico del popolo* with the title "Buna Lager." Levi changed the title to "Buna" when he published it along with other poems from that period in 1984 in a collection entitled *Ad un ora incerta*, a title borrowed from Coleridge's *At an Uncertain Hour*. Firmly establishing his subject position as a survivor who writes about his lost companions and his complicated relation to them, "Buna" speaks directly to the ways in which shame, autobiography, and testimony are mutually dependent.

Even though they engage similar themes, the differences between this 1945 poem and a much later work, his 1984 poem "The Survivor," discussed in chapter 4, reflect a dramatically changed perspective on Levi's part. In "Buna," he is also haunted by the memory of those dead companions, but his characterization of them is strikingly dissimilar to that in the later poem:

> Piedi piagati e terra maledetta,
> Lunga la schiera nei grigi mattini.
> Fuma la Buna dai mille camini,
> Un giorno come ogni giorno ci aspetta.

Terribili nell'alba le sirene:
"Voi moltitudine dai visi spenti,
Sull'orrore monotono del fango
È nato un altro giorno di dolore."
Compagno stanco ti vedo nel cuore,
Ti leggo gli occhi compagno dolente.
Hai dentro il petto freddo fame niente
Hai rotto dentro l'ultimo valore.
Compagno grigio fosti un uomo forte,
Una donna ti camminava al fianco.
Compagno vuoto che non hai più nome,
Un deserto che non hai più pianto,
Così povero che non hai più male,
Così stanco che non hai più spavento,
Uomo spento che fosti un uomo forte:
Se ancora ci trovassimo davanti
Lassù nel dolce mondo sotto il sole,
Con quale viso ci staremmo a fronte?
28 dicembre 1945

Wounded feet and accursed land
The line long in the gray mornings
Buna smokes from a thousand chimneys
A day like every other is waiting for us
Dreadful sirens at dawn
"You, crowds of lifeless faces
In the monotonous horror of the mud
Another day of pain is born."
Tired companion, I see you in my heart
I read your eyes, sad companion
You have in your breast cold, hunger, nothingness
Within you have lost all your worth
Gray companion, you were a strong man
A woman used to walk at your side
Empty companion who no longer has a name
Deserted, with no more tears
So impoverished there is no more pain
So tired there is no more fear
Lifeless man who was a strong man
If we were to find ourselves together again

Up there in the sweet world, under the sun
With what face would we stand before each other?[2]
28 December 1945

In the poem, the word *compagno*, companion, is repeated several times, emphasizing the close connection between the poet and those he writes about. The etymology of *compagno* is important to Levi's usage: from the medieval Latin, it signifies the person who eats bread with someone else. In this context, the figure of the *compagno* is deeply ironic, as a poem about camp prisoners is also always about starvation, bread-breaking with another person being an impossible luxury.[3]

The feel of the poem, from the outset, is quite different from that of "The Survivor." Recounted in the present tense, it draws the reader to imagine the place, with no distance of time to separate us from what is being described; as he says, "wounded feet and accursed land / The line long in the gray mornings / Buna smokes from a thousand chimneys / A day like every other is waiting for us." In this first part of the poem, Levi tellingly uses the plural pronoun to describe the prisoners: he is one of them, and this discursive act pulls the reader in very close. At the onset, there is little distance between himself and the other prisoners.

The next part of the poem engages the other prisoners as subjects: "you, crowds of lifeless faces." Yet the potential separation implied by the "you," as opposed to the "us" of the beginning, is mediated by the next lines, "tired companion, I see you in my heart / I read your eyes, sad companion." These lines are quite different from his descriptions of the *Muselmänner* found in *Survival in Auschwitz*. The description as it unfolds in this poem is that of prisoners who have been broken, who will not survive, as he repeats the word *spento*, extinguished, worn out: *spento* can also mean extinct or dead. In other words, they are *Muselmännër* according to Levi's definition of the same. In contrast to what he says in *Survival*, "an emaciated man, head bowed and shoulders bent, on whose face and in whose eyes no trace of thought can be seen," Levi is able to read the eyes of the companion in "Buna."[4] It is the tensions and differences between what is *potentially* lifeless, a subject that can still speak for itself, as Levi reads the message in the eyes, and that which is *invariably* lifeless that are revealed by Levi's use of the word *spento*.

In this poem, Levi draws no clear distinctions between those he describes and himself, except in the potential shame of survival, as he says, "If we were to meet again / Up there in the world, sweet beneath the sun, / With what kind of face would we confront each other?" The broken man is not being observed and commented upon with trepidation and distance. Instead the face, Janus-like, turns both ways, as the submerged looks at Levi and Levi looks at him. The gaze is postulated without the hostility and distance that characterizes Levi's descriptions of the submerged elsewhere. The tone of the last section in particular is markedly different than in "The Survivor," in which both accusation and distance are apparent, as he writes in that poem, "Stand back, away from here, submerged people, / Go away."

Antony Rowland has pointed out in his reading of "Buna" that the text functions as both poetry and testimony. He comments as well that "in 'Buna' the various ways in which the narrator addresses and describes the inmate illustrate the difficulties Levi experiences in writing about the *muselmann*."[5] Overall, however, the different modes of description in "Buna" are more similar than dissimilar, as speaker and subject embrace a common humanity and grieve its loss. That very loss creates distance between Levi and the figure of the submerged, yet it is a different kind of distance than has been noted elsewhere, what I will call a "close" distance, one that embraces rather than rejects.

The image of the "wounded feet" of the first line is particularly striking, as it simultaneously evokes the concepts of plagues, stigmata, and sacrifice. *Piaga* has a strong biblical connection in the Italian tradition, as it crosses over from the Judaic text, *le piaghe d'Egitto* (the plagues of Egypt) referring to the liberation of the Jews from the Pharaoh, part of the rites of Passover, to the Christian, *le sante piaghe di Cristo* (the holy wounds or stigmata of Christ). The mark of difference of the wounded feet also evokes Oedipus: the indelible sign that will foretell an impossible and painful future.

Through addressing the topic of the *Muselmänner*, "Buna" directly engages the topics of shame and of the subject position of the survivor in the post-Shoah era. The poem also speaks to the crisis of autobiography that we have seen in Levi's other works, as the first-person speaker of the poem cannot move forward without addressing his dead companions and the shame found within. Those themes so apparent in "Wstawac," his poem discussed in chapter 4 regarding the inescapability of the survivor's condition, are signalled in this very early work as well, yet with a radically different outcome. Levi's early poem "Buna" engages the themes that will remain at the heart of his opus. But when this poem is compared to his later work, it denotes deep and significant changes in his perspective that took place over his writing career of approximately forty years. Some of those changes are apparent within even a very short time frame, as his view of the *Muselmänner* in *Survival in Auschwitz* is quite different than what is apparent in "Buna."

One can only speculate as to the reasons for Levi's apparent change of heart regarding the submerged, the *Muselmänner*, in his other works. His modification of perspective is, I believe, an outcome of exposure to shame regarding the survivor's condition both immediately post-war and over time. The effect of this exposure is the greater distancing that Levi achieves in his other works in which the *Muselmänner* are discussed. Elspeth Probyn writes that Levi's legacy is crucial because he is "the writer who ensured that the shame of the Holocaust would outlive him ... he is the writer most associated with making us *feel* that shame is intrinsic to both humanity and inhumanity."[6] For Probyn, shame often carries a positive valence, because it is important for reminding us who we are; and for Levi, "the experiences of shame are also what reminds him of his humanity."[7]

There is a second early poem that is also relevant to understanding the changes in Levi's perspective regarding survival, as well as understanding the transformation of experience into literature and what the stakes were in such a move. Levi wrote this poem right after his return to Turin, an extremely powerful, elliptical, and very short piece entitled "February 25, 1944" that differs significantly from his other poetry and his work in general.

The poem speaks directly to a deep, personal anguish over the loss of his dear companion Vanda Maestro.[8] They were deported together and she was murdered a few months after their arrival at Auschwitz. The date found in the title of the poem heartbreakingly refers to the last day she and Levi spent together on the deportation to Auschwitz.

25 febbraio, 1944
Vorrei credere qualcosa oltre,
Oltre che morte ti ha disfatta.
Vorrei poter dire la forza
Con cui desiderammo allora,
Noi già sommersi,
Di potere ancora una volta insieme
Camminare liberi sotto il sole.
9 gennaio 1946

February 25, 1944
I'd like to believe in something besides
Besides the death that undid you
I'd like to be able to say the force
With which we desired back then
We, the already submerged
To be able to walk together, one more time,
Free under the sun.
January 9, 1946[9]

The overarching sentiment of this poem is a yearning for a time when death was not his constant companion, when life could be as free as it was before, although even that freedom is circumscribed by his use of the word "submerged." The notion of freedom as exemplified by being able to walk under the sun is reworked from "Buna." In "Buna," freedom is circumscribed by the ambiguous condition of the survivor who must face his former companions; in this second poem, there is instead nostalgia for a freedom that was lost. The differences between who lived and who was lost are not clearly drawn in "February 25, 1944"; Levi has put little distance between the speaker of these lines and his friend that was murdered. The poem is much more personal than is common in Levi's opus. His anguish is clear and is evoked both directly and structurally. Belpoliti has commented that in Levi's works there is a distance between the narrating voice and the listener, but in this poem that distance is not apparent.[10]

The word "desire" is remarkable in this context, and even more so when paired with the verb *dire*, to speak, to say. Love's desire, strongly suggested by this line, has been turned into the desire to say or speak the force of this desire, or life itself. That life, already compromised, already "submerged," is at once a mourning of the lack of life and a desire to reanimate it through the force of emotions felt, but perhaps not expressed at the time. Levi's desire to speak, to reanimate, and ultimately to *believe* in a different fate is striking, and it is the passage between his experience and the narrating that can commemorate it that is marked by this transition. He seeks to reject death, reaching instead for expression ("dire"), and ultimately arrives at the questions and frustration that telling the story can generate. His choice of "disfatta" in relation to death is significant: *disfare* means to undo something that's done; when the terms are reversed, undone death is life.

Elisabetta Tarantino has pointed out the Dantean subtext to this particular line of the poem, found in canto 3 of the *Inferno*:

e dietro le venìa sì lunga tratta
di gente, ch'i' non averei creduto
che morte tanta n'avesse disfatta.

Behind it came so long a file of people
that I could not believe
death had undone so many.[11]

These lines can be read as emblematic of Levi's testimonial project, as the reader here takes on the role of Dante the pilgrim, compelled to think about the sheer number involved in genocide, how death has indeed undone them. The credibility of the enormous numbers ("ch'i' non averei creduto") is brought into sharp focus and evokes the challenge of Holocaust representation.[12]

We can read Levi's "dire la forza" as the desire for literature, for testimony, that will endure. I argue that his own subject position in this poem, as a *sommerso*, crosses the line between survivor, *Muselmann*, and the dead. It evokes as well the title of his last collection of essays published in 1986, *I sommersi e i salvati* ("The Submerged and The Saved," mistranslated in the English edition as *The Drowned and the Saved*). To be "submerged" is a liminal state: perhaps on the way to becoming *Muselmänner* but not there yet, and certainly not saved, which ironically refers to his subject position as a survivor. But at what price this survival?

Elie Wiesel comments on the project of turning testimony into literature, as well as the relationship between the survivor and the story that he tells: "the past belongs to the dead and the survivor does not recognize himself in the words linking him to them."[13] How Levi has articulated this very relationship is apparent in the changes over time in his view of the submerged other and his own position vis-à-vis that difficult personal survival and the tools necessary to ensure survival of the story. His negotiation of this delicate terrain is apparent in these two early poems. The second poem in particular raises the question of what is at stake for the narrating survivor: what is risked by telling the story? Why he employs more distance between the narrator and what is being narrated in the rest of his opus becomes clear when we consider the direct gaze found in "February 25, 1944," so unbearably pained and painful.

These poems illustrate how shame, testimony, and autobiography work in a complicated concert for Levi. They address as well the perils of survival and those associated with telling the story. The importance of Levi's poetry as the expression of deeply felt sentiment is underscored by Levi himself in an interview in which he said that "poetry was more suitable than prose" for expressing that which was weighing on him.[14] Levi's theory of writing emerges from moments in which he negotiates narrative risk regarding Holocaust representation. He explores the concern that looking directly at the Holocaust can incur grave peril, expressed in his use of the trope of the Medusa and in other moments as well, as I have outlined in chapter 3. Irving Howe has argued that "cannier" writers have adopted the strategy of using Perseus's shield to look at the Holocaust, rather than employing a direct and therefore dangerous gaze:

> Perseus would turn to stone if he were to look directly at the serpent-headed Medusa, though he would be safe if he looked at her only through a reflection in a mirror or shield (this latter strategy, as I shall argue, being the very one that the cannier writers have adopted in dealing with the Holocaust).[15]

Another figure that has been used to expressing the danger in looking directly at the Holocaust is that of Lot's wife. Looking at this figure in relation to Levi's use of the Medusa provides a way to further appreciate his negotiation of various writerly identities through the terrain of a difficult survival.

The story of Lot's wife boldly illustrates what is at stake in the act of approaching the Holocaust, as it involves questions of why and how to witness, as well as the risks of recounting that witnessing. The story also stresses the ways in which shame, both ours and the survivor's, can be intermingled with the trauma of the historical event and with the enterprise of its narration. The tale of Lot's wife has fascinated readers, theologians, artists, and critics alike. Often cited as an infamous example of disobedience, she is left unnamed, unsung, and as objectified as that pillar of salt she became. The story has had very long legs, as her fate has repeatedly been used as a cautionary tale, particularly in Christian literature, to warn against defiance and to promote the idea of obedience and compliance. In her de-figuration into salt, she has become a figure for dehumanization, a lesson to those who would disobey, especially women.[16]

Wiesel also sees the story of Lot's wife as a cautionary tale, but in a radically different way. He raises troubling questions that are pertinent to the situation of Levi as a survivor and writer as he asks what it means to look at the Holocaust as an intellectual diversion, a topic that can be studied coldly and dispassionately. Vehemently rejecting cold approaches to the topic, which are neither commemorative nor respectful of those that died, Wiesel writes: "The future frightens us, the past fills us with shame ... and Lot's apprehensive wife, she was right to look back and not to be afraid to carry the burden of doomed hope."[17] He reads Lot's wife's decision as a significant prophetic and prescriptive moment. Within the hermeneutic framework that Wiesel sets up for understanding its importance, the action of Lot's wife speaks to the necessity of looking back in order to move forward, of understanding the imperative of looking at destruction as part of a principled worldview that insists on reflections on the past. In Wiesel's analysis, Lot's wife becomes a courageous figure that represents ethical choice and its consequences. From this point of view, the absolute commandment not to look is not only impossible for her, but also morally wrong.

Lot's wife has but one moment of agency, and she chooses to use this moment to look back at the past. She follows the urgency of an ethical gaze, but there is a steep price to pay. Because of this looking, she is dramatically deprived of the possibility of witnessing and testifying. The story of Lot's wife, then, read from a post-Shoah perspective, is not only about the necessity of confronting the past but also about the nature of witnessing. As Henry Knight says, we can see "the figure of Lot's wife as a positive valence for witnessing: the look at the Gorgon not as a nihilistic enterprise, but rather a step in the direction of an identity politics that embraces our troubled past."[18] She becomes a figure not for guilt, as guilt concerns actions, but for shame, for what she has become in the eyes of others, as her physical remnant is left for all to see. The figure of Lot's wife is an exemplar of the important differences between shame and guilt.

In his recovery of the figure of Lot's wife, Wiesel has brought her forward as an ethical model, but he has also put forward an even more radical idea by pairing her with shame and simultaneously rejecting the concept of her as shamed. This is consonant with Probyn's reading of shame as a positive force, especially in the works of Levi. Wiesel rejects the shaming that has been brought upon her, and repositions the shame of the Shoah where it more appropriately belongs, onto the society that allowed the Shoah to happen. This repositioning brings to light a central concern in the consideration of shame: its ability to involve whoever witnesses it.

The figure of Lot's wife has been recovered from the shame assigned to her, and validated instead as a witness to destruction who must look. She is a witness who has been forever silenced, and is a reminder to us to study the destruction, as she chose witnessing over silence, thus simultaneously becoming a figure for witnessing and for shame. Her figure encompasses the themes of witnessing, testimony, and shame, as well as identity positioning. Following Wiesel's prescription, she is recovered out of shame's arena, as that very shame was assigned because of her fatal insistence on witnessing. Wiesel's analysis is radically enabling: she can be understood as valiant rather than shamed, and the shame is repositioned where it more properly belongs.

The paradox of a figure that simultaneously stands for shame and for witnessing is highly relevant to this study of Levi. The shame that is evoked, negated, and repositioned through the figure of Lot's wife provides a way of thinking about two central concerns found in Levi's work that I discussed in chapter 5: his concept of survivor shame and its relationship to witnessing. In considering the ethical model of Lot's wife that Wiesel proposes, we might well ask ourselves if we can do as well in understanding the shame permeating the writing of Primo Levi, and make a similar recuperative gesture of repositioning. In what ways is the study of shame central to an understanding of Levi? What is at stake in the uncomfortable juxtaposition of shame and Holocaust testimony? It is precisely the tensions between witnessing and shame that are fruitful to explore: are they inevitably linked? Can one exist without the other? Levi's statement "We are the ones who, because of our transgressions, ability, or luck, did not touch bottom. The ones who did, who saw the Gorgon, did not come back to tell, or they came back mute,"[19] explored in the last chapter, is particularly relevant to his theory of the relation of witnessing to narration.

The tale of Lot's wife and how it can be posited as an ethical model in Holocaust representation can be compared to Levi's use of the Medusa as a metaphor for the evil of the Shoah and what happened to the "real" witnesses. Even though both are metaphors for the consequences of looking, they are different: the Gorgon has the face that can turn others to stone; Lot's wife is the face that was turned to stone. She is used as an example of the consequences of looking, the Gorgon is a warning of what will happen if looking takes place: yet both are figures for the consequences of a gaze. In Levi's use of the Gorgon in this passage, the stakes are as high as they were for Lot's wife, as looking means loss of life and therefore loss of witnessing. If the witnessing self cannot survive the actual witnessing, at what peril does this place the testimonial project? How does the relationship between autobiography, witnessing, and shame ultimately play out in relation to specularity? The distance that Levi posits between himself and those who did not make it is highly relevant to these concerns.

In Levi's lexicon, the three are inextricably entwined. In a sense, the survivors are all Lot's wives, paralysed by what they have seen. The "true witness" cannot return or returns mute; the *Sonderkommando*, who had the most information about the horrors of the camp and mass murder, become the Medusa if they speak factually about what they have witnessed. Autobiography is only possible under certain, very limited, conditions, and poses a threat to witnessing and testimony because of its emphasis on the individual rather than on the fate of the group. Announcing the threat of the Medusa, the Furies represent the permanent state of the survivor, as Levi comments: "the Furies, in whom we are forced to believe."[20] The "we" that Levi uses is indicative of that need to speak for the entire group: that testimony must incorporate the historicized account. Witnessing and testimony may be acts performed by individuals, but they come to embody the whole, speaking for all survivors.

Finally, how does witnessing work within the epistemological parameters that Levi sets up for it? If "true" witnessing cannot take place, as he states in "Shame," is he then making the case for literature to subsume that role, even at the risk of potentially inappropriate models? Levi conjectures the act of witnessing through his choice of trope regarding the danger of representation in witnessing. In effect, he theorizes witnessing every time he uses a cultural model – Dante chief among his referents – to employ or gloss that witnessing. Literature becomes his refuge: a way of addressing painful issues without looking at them too directly. His early poetry, as I have discussed, explores the risk of too close a gaze.

Levi's writing speaks to the necessity of witnessing, and to the painful necessity of at the same time mitigating the gaze of Medusa, through a careful and strategic narration. The interplay between his theories and practice of witnessing, autobiography, and shame form the core of his thought, and his various cultural identities play a crucial role in his choices regarding the ways in which he narrates his "ghastly tale."

Notes

1. Introduction

1 An example of this response to Levi can be found in Berel Lang's intellectual biography of Levi, where he refers to Levi as a "natural philosopher combining an intuition of significant theoretical questions underpinning historical practice with a keen sense of where responses to them can (*or* cannot) be found" (*Primo Levi*, 114). Lang's acutely perceptive assessment of Levi goes far beyond the usual assessments of Levi's work.

2 Druker, *Primo Levi and Humanism*, 2.

3 Young, *Writing and Rewriting the Holocaust*, 9–10.

4 For an excellent review of Levi's reception by critics, as well as close readings of his texts, see Sodi, *Narrative and Imperative*. See also Sodi and Marcus, introduction to *New Reflections on Primo Levi*.

5 See for example Zimmerman, *Jews in Italy*, for details on these episodes. Many members of the Italian Jewish community embraced fascism, especially early on, but even this political allegiance was often motivated by a deep patriotism.

6 The topic of irony in Levi's work has been explored most fruitfully and extensively by Robert Gordon in *Primo Levi's Ordinary Virtues*.

7 Druker, "Trauma and Latency," 64.

8 Quoted in Gilmore, *The Limits of Autobiography*. Another pertinent citation from Foucault is: "A work is definitely not the form of expression of a particular individuality. The work always implies, as it were, the death of the author. One only writes in order to disappear at the same time" ("Interview avec Michel Foucault," 660, passage translated by Clare O'Farrell).

9 Langer, *Admitting the Holocaust*, 13–24.

10 Wiesel, *Night*, 115.
11 Portnoff, "Levi's Auschwitz and Dante's Hell," 79.
12 Langer, "Interpreting Survivor Testimony," 26–40.
13 Hilberg, "I Was Not There," 23.
14 Wiesel, "A Plea for the Dead," 73, 77.
15 Levi, *The Drowned and the Saved*, 1.
16 English translations of Levi are from *Complete Works* (here, Kindle locations 35705–6).

2. The Complications of Jewish Identity

1 Levi, *Complete Works*, Kindle locations 12486–9.
2 For a more in-depth treatment of the construction of Jewish identity in Italy, see my "The Itinerary of an Identity." Some of that discussion is expanded and re-elaborated in this chapter.
3 Ian Thomson in *Primo Levi* discusses Levi's success with his exams during his first years at the university that allowed him to stay in the program; see chap. 6.
4 For a historically contextualized discussion of this issue, see Gilman, *The Jew's Body*.
5 Susan Zuccotti discusses the Racial Laws of 1938–39 and their impact on the lives of Jews in Italy in her *The Italians and the Holocaust*. See also Kertzer, *The Pope and Mussolini*.
6 Ian Thomson, *Primo Levi*, 98–9.
7 The historian Renzo de Felice is another figure of Levi's generation who tended to exculpate fascism and the role played by fascist antisemitism in the Holocaust. One may speculate that his reasons were similar to Levi's and to the young Arnaldo Momigliano's.
8 For a discussion regarding the construction of Jewish identity in Italy, see Harrowitz, "The Itinerary of an Identity."
9 Levi, *Complete Works*, Kindle locations 37584–6.
10 The remainder of this chapter relies on my essay "Primo Levi and Jewish Identity," but is heavily revised and extended.
11 Lang, "The Phenomenal-Noumenal Jew," 279.
12 Lang, "The Phenomenal-Noumenal Jew," 282.
13 Hook, "On Being a Jew," 34. Hook's definition is discussed in Goldstein, "Thoughts on Jewish Identity," 79–92.
14 There are three essays on Levi and Jewishness that are exemplars of these approaches: see Mendel's "Primo Levi and the Jews," 61–73; Sungolowsky, "The Jewishness of Primo Levi," 75–86; and Parussa, "A Hybridism of

Sounds," 87–94. Mendel's approach primarily looks at Levi's Jewish
identity within the unique context of Italian Jewishness; Sungolowsky
considers the way Levi thematizes Jewishness within his works; and
Parussa analyses the ways in which Levi's thought might be seen as
interacting with Jewish cultural and philosophical traditions.

15 Secular Judaism, sometimes also called cultural Judaism, is often defined
as a bond with Jewish tradition and culture that creates a Jewish identity
that is not religious in nature. Traditions may be followed according to
the individual's preference, but religious observation is a matter of choice
rather than of spiritual conviction. For a detailed discussion, see Malkin,
Secular Judaism.

16 Thomson, *Primo Levi*, 41.

17 See Hyman, *Gender and Assimilation*, and Reiter, "Karl Kraus and the
Jewish Self Hatred Question," for discussions of Jewish assimilation in
Europe.

18 For an excellent discussion of the inherent problems in the term
"assimilation," see Hyman, *Gender and Assimilation*, in particular chapter 1.

19 Thomson, *Primo Levi*, 408.

20 Cheyette, "Appropriating Primo Levi," 67–85.

21 For more information on the Manifesto della razza, see Zuccotti, *The
Italians and the Holocaust.*

22 See Zuccotti, *The Italians and the Holocaust*, for more information on the
racial laws and their consequences for the Italian Jewish community.

23 See Fabre, *Mussolini razzista* and *Il contratto.*

24 Cohen, "Consider if This Is a Man," 41.

25 Interview with Edith Bruck, in Gordon, *Voice of Memory*, 263.

26 Interview with Gad Lerner, in Gordon, *Voice of Memory*, 292.

27 Cheyette, "Appropriating Primo Levi."

28 Butler, in *Parting Ways*, discusses only part of Levi's statements on Israel
and ignores his belief that Israel needs to be defended.

29 See Levi's essays on writing and chemistry, "The Language of Chemists
I and II," in *Other People's Trades*, for his account of how being a chemist
influenced his writing style.

30 Giuliani, *A Centaur in Auschwitz*, 65.

31 Parussa, *Writing as Freedom*, 90.

32 As quoted in Giuliani, *A Centaur in Auschwitz*. The interview was
originally published in Poli and Calcagno, *Echi di una voce perduta*, 281.

33 Quoted in Giuliani, *A Centaur in Auschwitz*, 67; Poli and Calcagno, *Echi di
una voce perduta*, 281.

34 Belpoliti and Gordon, *The Voice of Memory*, 275.

35 Interview with Edith Bruck in Gordon, *The Voice of Memory*, 262.
36 For a discussion of Levi's marginalization, see Tosi, review of *New Reflections on Primo Levi*, 133–4.
37 In the original Hebrew, an accent is not used in the word *Sh'ma*, also spelled *Shema*, while in Italian an accent is used. I have maintained this distinction.
38 Translation mine.
39 Parussa, *Writing as Freedom*, 144.
40 Translation found at http://www.chabad.org/library/article_cdo/aid/706162/jewish/Translation.htm
41 Parussa, *Writing as Freedom*, 143.
42 The published translation of Levi's poem contains an error: *comandare* is translated as "commend" rather than "command," which has led to some unfortunate misreadings of the poem. See Rowland, "Poetry as Testimony," for a discussion.
43 Levi, *Opere*, 126.
44 Levi, *Complete Works*, Kindle locations 2496–2502.
45 Levi, *Complete Works*, Kindle location 2888.
46 Levi, *Opere*, 758.
47 Levi, *Complete Works*, Kindle locations 12313–15.
48 Cavaglion, *Notizie su Argon*, 2. Translation mine.
49 Giuliani, *A Centaur in Auschwitz*, 68.
50 Levi, *Complete Works*, Kindle locations 12030–3.
51 Levi, *Complete Works*, Kindle locations 12038–43.
52 Levi, *Complete Works*, Kindle locations 12048–53, 12059.
53 Levi, *Complete Works*, Kindle locations 12117–22.
54 Levi, *Complete Works*, Kindle locations 12148–64.
55 Levi, *Complete Works*, Kindle locations 12064–6.
56 http://www.etimo.it/; translation mine.
57 Levi, *Complete Works*, Kindle locations 12262–4.
58 For a discussion of this painful episode, see Thomson, *Primo Levi*, 7–13.
59 It is not clear exactly what Levi knew or did not know about the particulars of this episode: it appears that the older family members did not discuss it willingly, which in itself can be taken as emblematic of their desire to ignore anti-Jewish sentiment. See Angier, *The Double Bond*, for a more imaginative version of events and Thomson, *Primo Levi*, for more detail.
60 Camon, *Conversations with Primo Levi*, 68.
61 For discussions of Mussolini's antisemitic policies, see Fabre, *Il contratto*, and Zuccotti, *The Italians and the Holocaust*.

3. Primo Levi's Writerly Identity: From Science to Storytelling

1 For more details, see Thomson, *Primo Levi*.
2 Tosi, review of *New Reflections on Primo Levi*, 133–4.
3 Bravo, *Raccontare per la storia*, chap. 1.
4 White, "Figural Realism," 115–16.
5 Thomson, *Primo Levi*, 223–4.
6 See Gordon, *Voice of Memory*, xiii–ix.
7 Camon, *Conversations*, 41–2.
8 Gordon, *Voice of Memory*, 161.
9 De Benedetti and Levi, *Auschwitz Report*, 54.
10 De Benedetti and Levi, *Auschwitz Report*, 14.
11 De Benedetti and Levi, *Auschwitz Report*, 14.
12 Cavaglion, "Leonardo ed io," 64, translation mine.
13 In his critical introduction to the report, Robert Gordon has commented on the importance of this text in the composition of *Survival in Auschwitz*.
14 Robert Gordon, "Per mia fortuna," 337.
15 Levi, *Complete Works*, Kindle locations 705–11.
16 Levi, *Complete Works*, Kindle locations 942–7.
17 One notable exception is the work of Alberto Cavaglion, who has published a heavily annotated edition of *Se questo é un uomo* with frequent glosses on Levi's use of literary models, an edition that is a tour de force in its own right.
18 Howe, "Writing about the Holocaust," 186.
19 Ozick, "Primo Levi's Suicide Note," 37, 46.
20 Cheyette, "The Ethical Uncertainty of Primo Levi," 271.
21 Scheiber, "The Failure of Memory," 225.
22 In *The Memory of the Offense*, a critical study of Levi by Judith Woolf, she gives the following reason for using Levi's works to explicate *Survival in Auschwitz*: "in the absence of a definitive body of criticism, Levi remains the best explicator of his own work" (http://www.troubador.co.uk/book_info.asp?bookid=3).
23 One important exception is the intellectual biography of Levi by Berel Lang, who discusses the contradictions and fictionalizations found in Levi's work in *Primo Levi: The Matter of a Life*. Lina Insana's excellent study of Levi and translation performs close readings of his work.
24 "Forse il torto della critica é la sua pretesa non tanto di capire come funzionano I testi di Levi, ma come funziona Levi" (Scarpa, "Chiaro/oscuro," 233).

25 There are notable exceptions to what I have stated. Franco Baldasso is one critic who has fruitfully explored the literariness of Levi's work; see his *Il cerchio di gesso*.

26 White, "Figural Realism," Kindle locations 3441–2.

27 White, "Figural Realism," 115–16.

28 See "Communication," in Levi, *The Drowned and the Saved*.

29 Levi, *Black Hole of Auschwitz*, 105.

30 Gordon, *Voice of Memory*, 41–2.

31 Gordon, *Voice of Memory*, 163.

32 Levi, *Black Hole of Auschwitz*, 104.

33 Gordon, *Voice of Memory*, 169.

34 Berel Lang points out what great passion it must have taken for Levi to write in this seemingly detached manner (*Primo Levi*, 83).

35 For a compelling discussion of this issue, see Young, "Interpreting Literary Testimony."

36 Hilberg, "I Was Not There," 21.

37 Lang, *Post-Holocaust*, 121. See also Lang, *Holocaust Representation*, chap. 1.

38 Lang, *Primo Levi*, 63.

39 Howe, "Writing about the Holocaust," 182.

40 Bernstein, "Narrating the Shoah," 339.

41 Strejilevich, "Testimony," 703.

42 Rowland, "Poetry as Testimony, 488.

43 Langer, "Interpreting Survivor Testimony," 26–40.

44 Portnoff, "Levi's Auschwitz and Dante's Hell," 79.

45 Scheiber also asserts in her compelling analysis that through his manipulation of the Dantean text as well as the lacunae in the story, Levi is constructing his ideal reader ("Attento, Pikolo, apri gli orecchi e la mente").

46 Levi, *Complete Works*, Kindle location 2235. A note on the translations of Dante in this work: when Levi cites from Dante in his text, I use the translation found in the *Collected Works*. When I cite Dante as an influence or indirect reference that Levi is making, I use the Robert Hollander and Jean Hollander translation.

47 Levi, *Complete Works*, Kindle location 2245.

48 Levi, *Complete Works*, Kindle location 2260.

49 Insana, *Arduous Tasks*, 112; Gordon, "Primo Levi: The Duty of Memory," 131–40.

50 Levi, *Complete Works*, Kindle locations 2261–2.

51 Levi, *Complete Works*, Kindle location 2262.

52 Levi, *Complete Works*, Kindle locations 2264–5.

53 Druker, *Primo Levi and Humanism*, 37.

54 Insana, *Arduous Tasks*, 109.

55 Langer, "Interpreting Survivor Testimony," 45.

56 Jonathan Druker, "The Shadowed Violence of Culture," 152–3, addresses the appearance of Ulysses in *Survival in Auschwitz* by looking at what the figure of Ulysses means historically and how that affects the meaning of Levi's text. He takes Langer to task for being overly concerned with the implied function of the citation of Dante as an escape from the world of the camp, as Langer asserts that Primo and Jean forget where they are under the pressure of Dante's persuasive language.

57 Levi, *Complete Works*, Kindle locations 2397–2402.

58 Sharon Portnoff has written, "Levi uses a work of literature to dramatize his inability to find his own words to describe the whole of his experience" ("Levi's Auschwitz and Dante's Hell," 79). Perhaps Dante's language, despite its beauty, can indeed be viewed as the new harsh language that Levi postulates is needed to represent the Shoah.

59 Levi, *Complete Works*, Kindle locations 2279–80.

60 Levi, *Complete Works*, Kindle locations 2265–8.

61 Levi, *Complete Works*, Kindle locations 2281–4.

62 Levi, *Complete Works*, Kindle locations 36517–19.

63 Langer, "The Survivor as Author," 142.

64 The English translation of many of Levi's science fiction tales is entitled *The Sixth Day and Other Tales*. They also appear in the new *Complete Works*.

65 This section is revised from my essay "Mon maître, mon monstre," in *Monsters in the Italian Literary Imagination*, 51–64.

66 Levi, *Complete Works*, Kindle locations 6626–35.

67 Levi, *Complete Works*, Kindle locations 30356–8.

68 Freccero, *Father Figures*, 6–7.

69 Levi, *Complete Works*, Kindle locations 7209–10.

70 Levi, *Complete Works*, Kindle location 7260.

71 Levi, *Complete Works*, Kindle locations 7274–7.

72 Levi, *Complete Works*, Kindle locations 7221–4; 7242–3.

73 Levi, *Complete Works*, Kindle locations 7297–7323.

74 Levi, *Complete Works*, Kindle locations 7326–7.

75 Levi, *Complete Works*, Kindle locations 7279–80, 7282.

76 Levi, *Complete Works*, Kindle locations 7284–7285.

77 Levi, *Complete Works*, Kindle location 7291.

78 *Purgatorio* 10, 121–6. Translation from Dante, *Purgatorio*, trans. Robert Hollander and Jean Hollander, http://etcweb.princeton.edu/dante/pdp/.

79 Mirna Cicioni has done an excellent reading of the story, calling it "a bitterly ironic recontextualization of Dante's admonishment to the souls

of the proud in the first storey of Purgatory, about the need for imperfect humankind to strive to become closer to divine perfection" (*Primo Levi*, 64–5).

80 See for example Pross, "Nazi Doctors, German Medicine," 32–52.

81 Huet, *Monstrous Imagination*, 1.

82 Levi, *Complete Works*, Kindle location 7314.

83 See Levi, introduction and the chapter entitled "The Gray Zone" in *The Drowned and the Saved*, for a discussion of collaboration. In the introduction Levi discusses the civilian collaboration of petty bureaucrats who sold crematoria and cyclone-B gas to the Nazi regime.

84 Cohen, *Monster Theory*, 4.

85 Levi, *Complete Works*, Kindle locations 7327–8.

86 Huet, *Monstrous Imagination*, 6.

87 Robert Proctor, among other historians, has documented what he calls "the well-established fact of medical complicity in Nazi crimes," in *Racial Hygiene*.

4. Against Autobiography

1   Druker, *Primo Levi and Humanism*, 8.

2   Gilmore, *The Limits of Autobiography*, 3.

3   Levi, *Complete Works*, Kindle locations 710–11.

4   Gilmore, *The Limits of Autobiography*, 6.

5   Portnoff, "The Canon, Historicism and the Holocaust."

6   Portnoff, "The Canon, Historicism and the Holocaust."

7   Levi, *The Black Hole of Auschwitz*, 103.

8   Thomson, *Primo Levi*, 303.

9   Levi, *Complete Works*, Kindle locations 3823–7.

10 Levi, *Complete Works*, Kindle locations 3924–5.

11 Franco Baldasso, *Il cerchio di gesso*, discusses the importance of the Hurbinek episode and Levi's reworking of it in his essay on communication in *The Drowned and the Saved*.

12 Levi, *Complete Works*, Kindle locations 35982–3.

13 Translation mine.

14 Portnoff, "Not in Our Stars," 199, 202.

15 Levi, *Complete Works*, Kindle Locations 6590–9.

16 Probyn, *Blush*, 153.

17 Levi, *Complete Works*, Kindle locations 1452–65.

18 This section is an extensive revision of material previously published in my "Autobiography and the Narrator."

19 Levi, *Complete Works*, Kindle locations 14951–3.
20 Levi, *Complete Works*, Kindle locations 14953–5.
21 Gordon, *Voice of Memory*, 91.
22 Nora, "Between Memory and History,"145–6.
23 Lollini, "Primo Levi and the Idea of Autobiography," 76–7.
24 Levi, *Complete Works*, Kindle locations 12667–9.
25 Levi, *Complete Works*, Kindle location 3925.
26 Levi, *Complete Works*, Kindle locations 14951–2.
27 http://www.inlibroveritas.net/oeuvres/938/la-pucelle-d-orleans. Translation mine.
28 Levi, *Opere*, 2:1414. Translation mine.
29 Translation mine.
30 Insana, *Arduous Tasks*, 74–5.
31 In an earlier (1800) printing of *Lyrical Ballads*, the "Argument" at the head of the poem speaks of "how the Ancient Mariner cruelly and in contempt of the laws of hospitality killed a Seabird" (Coleridge, Gardner, and Doré, *Annotated Ancient Mariner*, Kindle locations 2180–1).
32 Coleridge, Gardner, and Dore, *Annotated Ancient Mariner*, Kindle locations 596–9.
33 Coleridge, Gardner, and Dore, *Annotated Ancient Mariner*, Kindle location 594.
34 The source of the code name was Germany's acclaimed poet and playwright Johann Wolfgang von Goethe (1749–1832), who used the phrase to describe clandestine actions often concealed by fog and the darkness of night.
35 Dante, *Inferno*, canto 33, 129–41, trans. Robert and Jean Hollander (*The Divine Comedy*, book 1), Kindle locations 12700–728, Knopf Doubleday Kindle edition.
36 As Mirna Cicioni comments in her analysis of the Dantean subtext of the poem, "The recontexting, which adds the notion of betrayal to that of guilt and the notion of being only apparently alive to that of surviving, is chilling in the global context of Levi's writings" (*Primo Levi*, 133).

5. Shame's Identity

1 Levi, *Complete Works*, Kindle locations 1851–2.
2 Leys, *From Guilt to Shame*, 165.
3 Shapiro, "The Tortured, Not the Torturers," 1134.
4 Leys, *From Guilt to Shame*, 11.
5 Leys, *From Guilt to Shame*, 7.

6 Briefly stated, the mimetic responses involves identification of the victim with the perpetrator, a contaminating effect that results in the victim's trying if possible to obtain power by victimizing others. In antimimesis, the victim remains aloof. For a much more detailed discussion of the differences between these two approaches, see Ley's introduction to *From Guilt to Shame*.

7 Leys, *From Guilt to Shame*, 6.

8 Wiesel, "A Plea for the Dead," 180.

9 Shapiro, "The Tortured, Not the Torturers," 1132.

10 Parussa, *Writing as Freedom*, 142.

11 Levi, *Complete Works*, Kindle location 36156.

12 Levi, *Complete Works*, Kindle locations 36409–11.

13 Levi, *Complete Works*, Kindle locations 36454–8.

14 Levi, *Complete Works*, Kindle locations 36467–8.

15 Levi, *Complete Works*, Kindle locations 35705–6.

16 Levi, *Complete Works*, Kindle locations 35675–6.

17 Levi, *Complete Works*, Kindle location 35932.

18 Levi, *Complete Works*, Kindle locations 36340–4.

19 Levi, *Complete Works*, Kindle locations 36550–4.

20 Farrell, "The Strange Case of the Muselmanner," 94.

21 For example, see Bruno Bettelheim and Robert Antelme, as discussed in Consonni, "Primo Levi, Robert Antelme."

22 Levi, *Complete Works*, Kindle locations 1887–90.

23 In Levi's discussion of the term, fatalism seems to be the most significant attribute of the *Muselmann*.

24 Joseph Farrell elaborates on the origin of the term in his essay "The Strange Case of the Muselmanner." For extensive discussion, see Ryn and Klodzinski, "An der Grenze Zwischen Leben und Tod."

25 Quoted in Consonni, "Primo Levi, Robert Antelme," 250–1. (The original text is found is Tedeschi, *Questo povero corpo*, 13–18; translation by Consonni.)

26 Ryn and Klodzinski, "An der Grenze Zwischen Leben und Tod," translation in Agamben, *Remnants of Auschwitz*, 42–3 (p. 94 in original text).

27 Consonni, "Primo Levi, Robert Antelme," 250.

28 Levi, *Complete Works*, Kindle locations 1175–7.

29 Levi, *Complete Works*, Kindle locations 1178–9.

30 Levi, *Complete Works*, Kindle locations 1183–5.

31 Levi, *Complete Works*, Kindle locations 1875–7.

32 Levi, *Complete Works*, Kindle locations 1906–8.

33 Levi, *Complete Works*, Kindle locations 1909–10.

34 Consonni, "Primo Levi, Robert Antelme," 244.

35 Consonni, "Primo Levi, Robert Antelme," 256.

36 Farrell, "The Strange Case of the Muselmanner."

37 Consonni, "Primo Levi, Robert Antelme," 252.

38 Rowland, "Poetry as Testimony," 493.

39 For an example of a glowing review of Agamben's text, see Bernstein's review, http://www.brynmawr.edu/bmrcl/Fall2002/Agamben.html.

40 Leys, *From Guilt to Shame*, 159–60. For more on this argument, see pp. 158–9.

41 Trezise, *Witnessing Witnessing*, 129.

42 Levi Della Torre, "Una nota critica al libro."

43 Agamben, *Remnants of Auschwitz*, 63–4.

44 Levi, *Complete Works*, Kindle locations 1897–8.

45 Secondary witnessing as a category has been fruitfully explored by Dora Apel in *Memory Effects*. Dominick LaCapra in *Writing History, Writing Trauma* also talks about secondary witnessing, as he discusses "the role of empathy and empathic unsettlement in the attentive secondary witness" (78).

46 Levi, *Complete Works*, Kindle locations 1889–90.

47 Levi, *Complete Works*, Kindle location 1907.

48 Agamben, *Remnants of Auschwitz*, 166.

49 Agamben, *Remnants of Auschwitz*, 166.

50 Agamben, *Remnants of Auschwitz*, 167–71.

51 Zdzislaw Ryn and Stanslaw Klodzinski, "An der Grenze zwischen Leben und Tod," 89–154. Passages translated in Agamben, *Remnants of Auschwitz*.

52 Mehlman, "Thoughts on Agamben's *Remnants of Auschwitz*," 13.

53 Filip Muller is the best-known of the survivors of the *Sonderkommando*. He has appeared in documentaries and has told his story many times, including his testimony *Eyewitness Auschwitz: Three Years in the Gas Chambers* (1999). Another who has written on his experiences is Shlomo Venezia, *Inside the Gas Chambers: Eight Months in the Sonderkommando of Auschwitz* (2011).

54 Agamben, *Remnants of Auschwitz*, 41.

55 See Trezise, *Witnessing Witnessing*, 123–8, for an extended discussion of Agamben's possible motivations regarding this point.

56 Consonni, "Primo Levi, Robert Antelme," 244.

57 Farrell, "The Strange Case of the Muselmanner," 97. Farrell also states: "Levi agrees in *The Drowned and the Saved* that he had come to this conclusion after deep thought and reading the testimony of others, but this is a profound change of heart, for he had not worried unduly over the

memory of the *Muselmanner* in the earlier *If This Is a Man* ... Primo Levi, implicitly but forcefully, revised in *The Drowned and the Saved* the more forthright views he had accepted in *If This Is a Man*" (97–8).

58 Agamben, *Remnants of Auschwitz*, 52.

59 Levi, *Complete Works*, Kindle locations 1159–60.

60 Lang, "The Representation of Evil," 353.

61 Lang, "The Representation of Evil," 356–7.

62 For a discussion of Levi's use of Macbeth as a moral model for science in his science fiction tale "Versamina," see Harrowitz, "Primo Levi's Science as 'Evil Nurse.'"

63 Levi, *Complete Works*, Kindle locations 36152–4.

64 Levi, *Complete Works*, Kindle locations 36550–5.

65 Levi, *Complete Works*, Kindle locations 35786–7.

66 Dante, *The Inferno*, Kindle locations 3624–51.

67 Freccero, *Dante: The Poetics of Conversion*, 128. See also Mazzotta, *Dante, Poet of the Desert*, 275–94, for a discussion of the Medusa as heresy; and Fosca's commentary in the Dartmouth Dante project: http://dante.dartmouth.edu.

68 *The Medusa Reader*, ed. Marjorie Garber and Nancy J. Vickers (New York: Routledge, 2003), p. 1.

69 It has been argued that Athena's punishment was perhaps no punishment at all; that instead she empowered Medusa by giving her the wherewithal to slay her enemies.

70 Dumoulié, "Medusa," 779.

71 Gilmore, *The Limits of Autobiography*, 7.

72 Dumoulie, "Medusa," 779.

73 Consonni, "Primo Levi, Robert Antelme," 256.

74 Knight, "From Shame to Responsibility," 56.

75 Levi, *Complete Works*, Kindle locations 36575–9.

76 Levi, *Complete Works*, Kindle location 36579.

77 From "Potassium," *The Periodic Table*, in *Complete Works*, Kindle locations 12819–22.

6. Conclusion: Cautionary Tales: Early Poetry

1 Buna was the name of one of the work camps within the Auschwitz complex.

2 Translation mine. There are published translations, one by Ruth Feldman and Brian Swann (*The Collected Poems of Primo Levi*), the other by Jonathan Galassi (*Complete Works*), but while certainly more poetic than my effort,

neither is completely faithful to the original. For example, in the other translations of this poem, the word *compagno*, repeated several times in the original, is translated using several different English words: "friend," "companion," "comrade." Yet the repetition of the same word is important in understanding Levi's intent.

3 "*Companio* nom., comp. di *cŭm* 'con' e un deriv. di *pānis* 'pane'; propr. 'chi mangia il pane con un altro'": see http://www.garzantilinguistica.it/ricerca/?q=compagno.

4 *Complete Works*, Kindle locations 1909–10.

5 Rowland, "Poetry as Testimony," 84. He also comments that "the various approaches to the figure in 'Buna' indicate that *Musselmänner* are both beyond representation and only encountered *in* representation" (84).

6 Probyn, *Blush*, 149.

7 Probyn, *Blush*, 161.

8 Ian Thomson (*Primo Levi*, 158–69) discusses at some length their friendship and Levi's romantic feelings for her. They were deported at the same time and spent those horrific last days together with two other friends, Luciana Nissim and Franco Sacerdoti, on the train to Auschwitz in deplorable conditions. Levi alludes briefly to the confidences they shared in the first chapter of *Survival in Auschwitz*, as well as to her death, which he would have found out about later.

9 Translation mine. The Jonathan Galassi translation in the new edition of Levi in English is very poetic, but falters by using the word "drowned" when *sommersi* is clearly *not* this, but "submerged."

10 Belpoliti, "I Am a Centaur," xix.

11 Tarantino, "Primo Levi e il dolce mondo." The lines from Dante are from *Inferno*, canto 3, 55–7 (*The Divine Comedy*, book 1), trans. Robert Hollander and Jean Hollander (Knopf Doubleday, Kindle edition), Kindle locations 1472–7.

12 This passage occurs soon after Dante has passed through the gates of hell at the beginning of canto 3, leaving behind all hope. This circle is for the apathetic: those who lived without shame and without honour. Boccaccio does an interesting expository reading of the passage: "Giovanni Boccaccio (1373–75), *Inferno* 3.55–7

[*Esposizione litterale*] E dietro le venia, a questa insegna, sì lunga tratta, cioè sì gran quantità, Di gente, d'anime state di genti, ch'io non avrei creduto, avanti che io avessi veduto questo, Che morte tanta n'avesse disfatta, cioè uccisa. E dice disfatta, per ciò che la morte non è altro che la separazione dell'anima dal corpo, la quale per la morte separandosi, resta questa composizione dell'anima e del corpo, le quali insieme fanno l'uomo, essere disfatta; per ciò che, dopo cotale dipartimento, colui, che prima era uomo, non è poi più uomo." (And he says *disfatta* [undone], for death is nothing but the separation of the soul from the body, which separates because of death, and there remains this composite of soul and body, which together make the man, are undone, for which after such behaviour, he who was before a man, now is no longer a man.) Boccaccio's understanding of *disfatta* as a definition of death's separation of the soul from the body is quite compelling in the context of a discussion about the *Muselmänner*. See Boccaccio, Commentary, Dartmouth Dante Project.

13 Wiesel, "The Holocaust as Literary Inspiration," 7.
14 Nascimbeni, "Levi: L'ora incerta della poesia," 137.
15 Howe, "Writing about the Holocaust," 38.
16 A longer version of this section is elaborated in my essay "Lot's Wife and 'A Plea for the Dead.'"
17 Wiesel, "A Plea for the Dead," 180. The essay was written in response to the trial of Adolf Eichmann in Jerusalem in 1962, as well as the reactions to that trial, including Hannah Arendt's assessment of the banality of evil that came out of her observations of Eichmann.
18 Knight, "Extending the Great Intercession," 6.
19 *Complete Works*, Kindle locations 36551–3.
20 *Complete Works*, (Kindle locations 35786–7.

Bibliography

Agamben, Giorgio. *Remnants of Auschwitz: The Witness and the Archive*. Trans. Daniel Heller-Roazen. New York: Zone, 2002.

Angier, Carol. *The Double Bond: The Life of Primo Levi*. New York: Farrar, Straus and Giroux, 2002.

Apel, Dora. *Memory Effects: The Holocaust and the Art of Secondary Witnessing*. New Brunswick: Rutgers University Press, 2002.

Baldasso, Franco. *Il cerchio di gesso: Primo Levi, narrator e testimone*. Bologna: Edizioni Pendagon, 2007.

Belpoliti, Marco. "I Am a Centaur." Preface to *The Voice of Memory: Interviews 1961–1987*, edited by Marco Belpoliti and Robert Gordon, xvii–xxii. New York: Polity, 2001.

Belpoliti, Marco, and Robert Gordon, ed. *The Voice of Memory*. New York: Polity, 2001.

Bernstein, Michael Andre. "Narrating the Shoah." In *A Holocaust Reader*, edited by Michael L. Morgan, 337–49. Oxford: Oxford University Press, 2000.

Bernstein, Richard J. Review of Giorgio Agamben, *Remnants of Auschwitz*. *Bryn Mawr Review of Comparative Literature*, 3, no. 2 (Fall 2002). http://www.brynmawr.edu/bmrcl/Fall2002/Agamben.html.

Boccaccio, Giovanni. Commentary on *Inferno* 3.55–7. Dartmouth Dante Project, https://dante.dartmouth.edu/search_view.php?doc=137351030550&cmd=gotoresult&arg1=16.

Bravo, Anna. *Raccontare per la storia/Narratives for History*. Milan: Einaudi, 2014.

Butler, Judith. *Parting Ways: Jewishness and the Critique of Zionism*. New York: Columbia University Press, 2012.

Camon, Ferdinando. *Conversations with Primo Levi*. Marlboro: Marlboro Press, 1989.

Cavaglion, Alberto. "'Leonardo ed io, in un silenzio gremito di memoria': Sopra una fonte dimenticata di *Se questo é un uomo*." In *Primo Levi: Memoria e Invenzione, Atti del convegno internazionale*, edited by Giovanna Ioli, 64–84. San Salvatore Monferrato: Edizioni della Biennale, 1995.

– *Notizie su Argon: Gli antenati di Primo Levi da Francesco Petrarca a Cesare Lombroso*. Turin: Instar Libri, 2006.

Cheyette, Bryan. "Appropriating Primo Levi." In *The Cambridge Companion to Primo Levi*, edited by Robert S.C. Gordon, 67–85. Cambridge: Cambridge University Press, 2007.

– "The Ethical Uncertainty of Primo Levi." In *Modernity, Culture and "The Jew,"* edited by Bryan Cheyette and Laura Marcus, 268–81. Stanford: Stanford University Press, 1998.

Cicioni, Mirna. *Primo Levi: Bridges of Knowledge*. Oxford: Berg, 1995.

Cohen, Joel. *Monster Theory: Reading Culture*. Minneapolis: University of Minnesota Press, 1993.

Cohen, Uri. "Consider if This Is a Man: Primo Levi and the Figure of Ulysses." *Jewish Social Studies: History, Culture, Society*, n.s. 18, no. 2 (2012): 40–69.

Coleridge, Samuel Taylor, Martin Gardner, and Gustave Doré. *Annotated Ancient Mariner: The Rime of the Ancient Mariner*. Prometheus Kindle edition, 2010.

Consonni, Manuela. "Primo Levi, Robert Antelme and the Body of the Musselmann." *Partial Answers: Journal of Literature and the History of Ideas*, 7, no. 2 (2009): 243–59.

Dante. *The Inferno*. Book 1 of *The Divine Comedy*. Translated by Robert Hollander and Jean Hollander. Knopf Doubleday, Kindle edition.

De Benedetti, Leonardo, and Primo Levi. *Auschwitz Report*. Edited by Robert Gordon. Translated by Judith Woolf. London: Verso, 2006.

Druker, Jonathan. *Primo Levi and Humanism after Auschwitz*. New York: Palgrave Macmillan, 2009.

– "The Shadowed Violence of Culture: Fascism and the Figure of Ulysses in Primo Levi's Survival in Auschwitz." *Clio: An Interdisciplinary Journal of Literature, History, and the Philosophy of History*, 33, no. 2 (2004): 143–61.

– "Trauma and Latency in Primo Levi's *The Reawakening*." In *New Reflections on Primo Levi: Before and After Auschwitz*, edited by Risa Sodi and Millicent Marcus, 63–77. New York: Palgrave MacMillan, 2011.

Dumoulié, Camille. "Medusa." In *Companion to Literary Myths, Heroes, and Archetypes*, edited by Pierre Brunel, 779–87. New York: Routledge, 1996.

Fabre, Giorgio. *Il contratto: Mussolini editore di Hitler, Mussolini razzista*. Bari: Dedalo, 2004.

– *Mussolini razzista: Dal socialismo al fascismo: La formazione di un antisemita*. Milan: Garzanti, 2005.Farrell, Joseph. "The Strange Case of the *Muselmänner* in Auschwitz." In *New Reflections on Primo Levi: Before and After Auschwitz*, edited by Risa Sodi and Millicent Marcus, 89–99. New York: Palgrave MacMillan, 2011.

Feldman, Ruth, and Brian Swann, trans. *The Collected Poems of Primo Levi*. Boston: Faber and Faber, 1988.

Foucault, Michel. "Interview avec Michel Foucault." In *Dits et Ecrits, 1954–1988*, vol. 3, 654–60. Paris: Gallimard, 1994.

Freccero, John. *Dante: The Poetics of Conversion*. Cambridge, MA: Harvard University Press, 1986.

Freccero, Carla. *Father Figures: Genealogy and Narrative Structure in Rabelais*. Ithaca: Cornell University Press, 1991.

Garber, Marjorie, and Nancy J. Vickers, eds. *The Medusa Reader*. New York: Routledge, 2003.

Gilman, Sander. *The Jew's Body*. New York: Routledge, 1991.

Gilmore, Leigh. *The Limits of Autobiography: Trauma and Testimony*. Ithaca: Cornell University Press, 2001.

Giuliani, Massimo. *A Centaur in Auschwitz: Reflections on Primo Levi's Thinking*. New York: Lexington, 2003.

Goldstein, Leon. "Thoughts on Jewish Identity." In *Jewish Identity*, edited by David Theo Goldberg and Michael Krausz, 79–92. Philadelphia: Temple University Press, 1993.

Gordon, Robert. "'Per mia fortuna ...': Irony and Ethics in Primo Levi's Writing." *Modern Language Review*, 92, no. 2 (1997): 337–47.

– *Primo Levi's Ordinary Virtues: From Testimony to Ethics*. Oxford: Oxford University Press, 2001.

– "Primo Levi: The Duty of Memory." In *European Memories of the Second World War*, edited by Helmut Peitsch, Charles Burdett, and Claire Gorrara, 131–40. New York: Berghahn, 2005.

–, ed. *Voice of Memory: Interviews, 1961–1987*. New York: Polity, 2001.

Harrowitz, Nancy. "Autobiography and the Narrator: Primo Levi's *Periodic Table*." In *Answering Auschwitz: Primo Levi's Science and Humanism After the Fall*, edited by Stanislao G. Pugliese, 177–90. New York: Fordham University Press, 2011.

– "The Itinerary of an Identity: Primo Levi's 'Parallel Nationalization.'" In *New Reflections on Primo Levi: Before and After Auschwitz*, edited by Risa Sodi and Millicent Marcus, 31–43. New York: Palgrave MacMillan, 2011.

- "Lot's Wife and 'A Plea for the Dead': Commemoration, Memory and Shame." In *Elie Wiesel: Jewish, Moral, and Literary Perspectives*, edited by Steven T. Katz and Alan Rosen, 103–12. Bloomington: Indiana University Press, 2013.
- "Mon maître, mon monstre." In *Monsters in the Italian Literary Imagination*, edited by Keala Jewell, 51–64. Detroit: Wayne State University Press, 2001.
- "Primo Levi and Jewish Identity: Strategies for Integration." In *Cambridge Companion to Primo Levi*, edited by Robert Gordon, 17–32. Cambridge: Cambridge University Press, 2007.
- "Primo Levi's Science as 'Evil Nurse': The Lesson of Inversion." In *Memory and Mastery: The Legacy of Primo Levi*, edited by Roberta Kremer, 59–73. New York: SUNY Press, 2001.

Hilberg, Raul. "I Was Not There." In *Writing and the Holocaust*, edited by Berel Lang, 17–25. New York: Holmes and Meier, 1988.

Hook, Sidney. "On Being a Jew." *Commentary*, 88, no. 4 (1989): 28–36.

Howe, Irving. "Writing about the Holocaust." In *Writing and the Holocaust*, edited by Berel Lang, 175–99. New York: Holmes and Meier, 1988.

Huet, Marie-Hélène. *Monstrous Imagination*. Cambridge, MA: Harvard University Press, 1993.

Hyman, Paula. *Gender and Assimilation*. Seattle: University of Washington Press, 1995.

Insana, Lina N. *Arduous Tasks: Primo Levi, Translation and the Transmission of Holocaust Testimony*. Toronto: University of Toronto Press, 2009.

Kertzer, David I. *The Pope and Mussolini: The Secret History of Pius XI and the Rise of Fascism in Europe*. New York: Random House, 2013.

Knight, Henry. "Extending the Great Intercession: Midrashic Reflections on Gen 18:20–33 and Matthew 7: 7–11." Unpublished manuscript of lecture presented at Valparaiso University, Valparaiso, IN, April 2004.

Knight, Henry F. "From Shame to Responsibility and Christian Identity: The Dynamics of Shame and Confession Regarding the Shoah." *Journal of Ecumenical Studies*, 35, no. 1 (1998): 41–62.

LaCapra, Dominick. *Writing History, Writing Trauma*. Baltimore: Johns Hopkins University Press, 2000.

Lang, Berel. *Holocaust Representation: Art within the Limits of History and Ethics*. Baltimore: Johns Hopkins University Press, 2000.

- "The Phenomenal-Noumenal Jew: Three Antinomies of Jewish Identity." In *Jewish Identity*, edited by David Theo Goldberg and Michael Krausz, 279–90. Philadelphia: Temple University Press, 1993.

– *Post-Holocaust: Interpretation, Misinterpretation, and the Claims of History*.
    Bloomington: Indiana University Press, 2005.
– *Primo Levi: The Matter of a Life*. New Haven: Yale University Press, 2014.
– "The Representation of Evil: Ethical Content as Literary Form." In *A
    Holocaust Reader: Responses to the Nazi Genocide*, edited by Michael L.
    Morgan, 349–58. Oxford: Oxford University Press, 2001.
Langer, Lawrence. *Admitting the Holocaust: Collected Essays*. New York: Oxford
    University Press, 1995.
– "Interpreting Survivor Testimony." In *Writing and the Holocaust*, edited by
    Berel Lang, 26–40. Teaneck, NJ: Holmes and Meier, 1984.
– "The Survivor as Author." In *New Reflections on Primo Levi: Before and After
    Auschwitz*, edited by Risa Sodi and Millicent Marcus, 133–47. New York:
    Palgrave McMillan, 2011.
Levi, Primo. *Black Hole of Auschwitz*. Edited by Marco Belpoliti. Translated by
    Sharon Wood. London: Polity, 2006.
– *The Complete Works of Primo Levi*. Edited by Ann Goldstein and translated by
    Jonathan Galassi. New York: Liveright, 2015.
– *The Drowned and the Saved*. Translated by Raymond Rosenthal. New York:
    Vintage, 1989.
– *I sommersi e i salvati*. Milan: Einaudi, 2003.
– *L'altrui mestiere (A Search for Roots)*. In *Opere*, vol. 2, edited by Marco
    Belpoliti. Turin: Einaudi, 1997.
– *Opere*. Edited by Marco Belpoliti. Turin: Einaudi, 1997.
– *Other People's Trades*. Abacus, 1990.
– *Se questo è un uomo*. Annotated edition, edited by Alberto Cavaglion. Milan:
    Giulio Einaudi, 2012.
– *The Sixth Day and Other Tales*. Translated by Raymond Rosenthal. London:
    Michael Joseph, 1990.
Levi Della Torre, Stefano. "Una nota critica al libro, *Quel che resta di
    Auschwitz*." *Una città*, no. 83, February 2000. Reprinted as appendix to Levi,
    I sommersi e i salvati.
Leys, Ruth. *From Guilt to Shame: Auschwitz and After*. Princeton: Princeton
    University Press, 2007.
Lollini, Massimo. "Primo Levi and the Idea of Autobiography." In *Primo Levi:
    The Austere Humanist*, edited by Joseph Farrell, 67–89. Oxford: Peter Lang,
    2003.
Malkin, Yaakov. *Secular Judaism: Faith, Values and Spirituality*. Vallentine
    Mitchell, 2003.
Mandelbaum, Allen. *Digital Dante*. http://dante.ilt.columbia.edu/comedy/.

Mazzotta, Giuseppe. *Dante, Poet of the Desert*. Princeton: Princeton University Press, 1979.

Mehlman, Jeffrey. "Thoughts on Agamben's *Remnants of Auschwitz*." Unpublished manuscript of talk presented at the University of Minnesota, 13 April 2011.

Mendel, David. "Primo Levi and the Jews." In *The Legacy of Primo Levi*, edited by Stanislao G. Pugliese, 61–73. New York: Palgrave Macmillan 2005.

Muller, Filip. *Eyewitness Auschwitz: Three Years in the Gas Chambers*. 1979. Reprint, Chicago: Ivan Dee, 1999.

Nascimbeni, Giulio. "Levi: L'ora incerta della poesia." Interview with Primo Levi. In *Primo Levi: Conversazioni e interviste, 1963–1987*, edited by Marco Belpoliti, 136–41. Milan: Einaudi, 1997.

Nora, Pierre. "Between Memory and History: Le Lieux de Mémoires." In *Theories of Memory*, edited by Michael Rossington and Anne Whitehead, 144–9. Baltimore: Johns Hopkins University Press, 2007.

Ozick, Cynthia. "Primo Levi's Suicide Note." In *Metaphor and Memory*, 37–46. New York: Alfred A. Knopf, 1989.

Parussa, Sergio. "A Hybridism of Sounds: Primo Levi between Judaism and Literature." In *The Legacy of Primo Levi*, edited by Stanislao G. Pugliese, 87–94. New York: Palgrave Macmillan 2005.

– *Writing as Freedom, Writing as Testimony: Four Italian Writers and Judaism*. Syracuse: Syracuse University Press, 2008.

Peitsch, Helmut, Charles Burdett, and Claire Gorrara, eds. *European Memories of the Second World War*. New York: Berghahn, 2005.

Poli, Gabriella, and Giorgio Calcagno, ed. *Echi di una voce perduta: Incontri, interviste e conversazioni con Primo Levi*. Milan: Mursia editore, 1992.

Portnoff, Sharon. "The Canon, Historicism and the Holocaust in Primo Levi's Memoirs," Paper presented at Association of Jewish Studies conference, Washington, DC, December 2011.

– "Levi's Auschwitz and Dante's Hell." *Culture and Society*, 46, no. 1 (2009): 76–84.

– "Not in Our Stars: Primo Levi's *Reveille* and Dante's *Purgatorio*." *Idealistic Studies*, 44: 198–208.

Probyn, Elspeth. *Blush: Faces of Shame*. Minneapolis: University of Minnesota Press, 2005.

Proctor, Robert. *Racial Hygiene: Medicine under the Nazis*. Cambridge: Harvard University Press, 1988.

Pross, Christian. "Nazi Doctors, German Medicine and Historical Truth." In *The Nazi Doctors and the Nuremberg Code*, edited by George J. Annas and Michael A. Grodin, 32–52. New York: Oxford University Press, 1992.

Rabelais, François. *The Complete Works of François Rabelais*. Translated by Donald M. Frame. Berkeley: University of California Press, 1991.

Reiter, Paul. "Karl Kraus and the Jewish Self Hatred Question." *Jewish Social Studies*, 10, no. 1 (2003): 78–116.

Rowland, Antony. "Poetry as Testimony: Primo Levi's Collected Poems." *Textual Practice*, 22, no. 3 (2008): 487–505.

Ryn, Zdzislaw, and Stanilsaw Klodzinski. "An der Grenze Zwischen Leben und Tod. Eine Studie über die Erscheinung des 'Muselmann' in Konzentrationslager." *Auschwitz-Hefte*, 1 (1987): 89–154.

Scarpa, Domenico. "Chiaro/oscuro." In *Riga*, vol. 13, edited by Marco Belpoliti, 230–53. Milan: Marcos y Marcos, 1997.

Scheiber, Elizabeth. "Attento, Pikolo, apri gli orecchi e la mente: Listening to Primo Levi's Holocaust Tales." *NeMLA Italian Studies* (Northeast Modern Language Association), 32 (2009–10): 111–28.

– "The Failure of Memory and Literature in Primo Levi's *Il sistema periodico*." *MLN*, 121 (2006): 225–39.

Shapiro, David. "The Tortured, Not the Torturers, Are Ashamed." *Social Research*, 70, no. 4 (2003): 1131–48.

Sodi, Risa. *A Dante of Our Time: Primo Levi and Auschwitz*. New York: Peter Lang, 1990.

– *Narrative and Imperative: The First Fifty Years of Italian Holocaust Writing, 1944–1994*. New York: Peter Lang, 2007.

Sodi, Risa, and Millicent Marcus, eds. *New Reflections on Primo Levi: Before and After Auschwitz*. New York: Palgrave MacMillan, 2011.

Strejilevich, Nora. "Testimony: Beyond the Language of Truth." *Human Rights Quarterly*, 28, no. 3 (2006): 701–13.

Sungolowsky, Joseph. "The Jewishness of Primo Levi." In *The Legacy of Primo Levi*, edited by Stanislao G. Pugliese, 75–86. New York: Palgrave Macmillan, 2005.

Tarantino, Elisabetta. "Primo Levi e il dolce mondo." http://www.academia.edu/3636568/Primo_Levi_e_il_dolce_mondo.

Tedeschi, Giuliana. *Questo povero corpo*. Milan: EDIT, 1946.

Thomson, Ian. *Primo Levi*. London: Random House, 2002.

Tosi, Giuseppe. Review of *New Reflections on Primo Levi: Before and After Auschwitz*, edited by Risa Sodi and Millicent Marcus. *Journal of Modern Italian Studies*, 18, no. 1 (2013): 133–4.

Trezise, Thomas. *Witnessing Witnessing: On the Reception of Holocaust Survivor Testimony*. New York: Fordham University Press, 2013.

Venezia, Shlomo. *Inside the Gas Chambers: Eight Months in the Sonderkommando of Auschwitz*. New York: Polity, 2011.

White, Hayden. "Figural Realism in Witness Literature." *Parallax*, 10, no. 1 (2004): 113–24.

Wiesel, Elie. "The Holocaust as Literary Inspiration." In Elie Wiesel, Lucy Dawidowicz, Dorothy Rabinowicz, and Robert McAfee Brown, *Dimensions of the Holocaust*, 5–11. Evanston: Northwestern University Press, 1990.

– *Night*. Translated by Marion Wiesel. New York: Hill and Wang, 2006.

– "A Plea for the Dead." In *Legends of Our Times*, 174–84. New York: Avon, 1968.

Woolf, Judith. *The Memory of the Offense: Primo Levi's If This Is a Man*. Leicester: Troubador, 2001.

Young, James. "Interpreting Literary Testimony: A Preface to Rereading Holocaust Diaries and Memoirs." *New Literary History* (special issue entitled *Literacy, Popular Culture, and the Writing of History*), 18, no. 2 (1987): 403–23.

– *Writing and Rewriting the Holocaust*. Bloomington: Indiana University Press, 1988.

Zimmerman, Joshua, ed. *Jews in Italy under Fascist and Nazi Rule: 1922–1945*. Cambridge: Cambridge University Press, 2005.

Zuccotti, Susan. *The Italians and the Holocaust: Persecution, Rescue, and Survival*. 2nd ed. Lincoln: University of Nebraska Press, 1996.

Index